Social Media Marketing in 2019

Strategies to Become an Influencer with Facebook, Instagram, Youtube and Twitter, Grow Your Personal Brand Fast in 2019 and Beyond

Jack Gary

of the work or a recorded copy and is only allowed with the express written consent from the Publisher. All additional rights reserved.

The information in the following pages is broadly considered a truthful and accurate account of facts and as such, any inattention, use, or misuse of the information in question by the reader will render any resulting actions solely under their purview. There are no scenarios in which the publisher or the original author of this work can be in any fashion deemed liable for any hardship or damages that may befall them after undertaking information described herein.

Additionally, the information in the following pages is intended only for informational purposes and should thus be thought of as universal. As befitting its nature, it is presented without assurance regarding its prolonged validity or interim quality. Trademarks that are mentioned are done without written consent and can in no way be considered an endorsement from the trademark holder.

Table of Contents

Introduction

People today interact with brands through social media. Therefore, having a strong social presence and being able to adequately tell the story of your brand is the key to creating empathy and loyalty. If implemented correctly, social media marketing can help your company achieve your growth and reputation goals.

What Is Social Media Marketing?

Social media marketing, or SMM, is a form of web marketing that uses a series of social media platforms in order to obtain a profitable and empathetic online advertising communication with users. Social media marketing retains users and customers by sharing textual content, images, and viral videos.

This book was created to provide useful information on social media marketing aimed at improving its business and giving businesses an operational tool with great advertising potentials at reduced costs. By reading this book, you can start developing your social media marketing plan in a more professional way.

Social Media and Marketing: Start with a Plan

Before starting to create a social media marketing campaign on Facebook, Instagram, YouTube, etc., you need to consider your sales and branding goals. Starting a social media marketing campaign without a strategic plan is like walking through a forest without a map — you will get lost.

Create a social media marketing plan and reflect on the goals to be achieved. What do you hope to achieve through social media marketing? What is your target audience? Where can you contact this target audience and how do you use social media? What message do you want to send to your target audience?

Social Media Marketing: Develop Goals

Social media marketing can help you achieve several goals such as:

- Increased traffic profiled towards your company website.
- Increase in leads and conversions.
- Increase of brand awareness.
- Creating a brand identity and a positive image of the brand (brand reputation).
- Communicate and interact empathically with your customers.

The Best Tips to Learn in Marketing with Social Media

Here are some social media marketing tips to get your bearings right during all social media campaigns.

Planning

As mentioned earlier, building a social media marketing plan is essential. It is necessary to identify the keywords, ideas, and contents that could be of interest to the target audience.

9

Content Is the Most Important Factor

As with other areas of online marketing, content is the most important thing when it comes to social media marketing. Be sure to provide interesting and viral information to your customers. Create different types of content using images, videos, and infographics, as well as classic content marketing.

Be Consistent

Using social media for marketing allows your company to advertise brands and products across a wide range of channels. Although each platform has its own unique environment, the core of your online communication must remain similar for all channels.

Blog

A blog is a great tool for social media marketing that allows you to share a wide range of information and valuable content for readers. Your company blog can also serve as a social media marketing blog, thus creating a place to highlight your company's activities.

Link

Although the use of social media for marketing is mainly based on the unique and original sharing of content concerning its business, in order to gain more fans and followers, it is also excellent for linking external articles. If other sources provide information that you think is valuable to your target audience, it is useful to create a dedicated link. The connection to external sources improves trust and reliability, and it is also possible to receive the same favor.

Keeping Track of Competitors

It's always important to keep an eye on your competitors who can provide valuable data on keyword searches, links to the business, and other important information. If your competitors are using a certain social media marketing technique that seems to work for them, you just have to do the same thing, but better.

Since Facebook stores data about its users which are entered spontaneously in their profile (e.g. age, location, interests), it has a very good idea of who its users are and what they are interested in. For example, just put a like on a football page to make them understand that you are following this sport. You will understand then that the potential of subjecting these well-defined users to targeted advertisements is enormous.

In the past years, social media has become one of the most effective advertising channels, is able to get new leads (contacts), and turn them into paying customers. Facebook Ads works in both B2C and B2B and there are many cases that show an increase in results, even 5 times, after taking advantage of advertising on Facebook.

The growth of Facebook is steady both in terms of new users and marketing opportunities. The budgets dedicated to the AD on social media have doubled worldwide in the last 2 years, from $16 billion in 2014 to $31 billion in 2016. In 2018, analysts expect a further increase of 26.3%.

To all of this, add that the number of active users every day on Facebook which was about 1.23 billion people in 2017 and on average, each of these spends 50 minutes a day between Facebook, Instagram, and Messenger. With Facebook Ads, you can reach each of these users with highly customizable targets such as interests, demographics, locations, actions performed on a website, and much more.

Do you own a small business and want to start a Social Media Marketing activity in 2019 to promote your business? If the answer is yes, below you will find 10 rules to follow to get success.

1) Do not improvise: Before opening your social accounts and starting to publish, analyze the target audience and based on its characteristics, realize a strategy that provides the guidelines to follow in all areas of communication, from the choice of channels to the definition of contents.

2) Give the public what they want: Create quality content, provide information, advice, and curiosity that can really interest and engage your audience.

13

3) Do not be too promotional: Avoid talking only about your company or your products. The goal of social networks is to create conversations; do not make classic advertising.

4) Interacting: Respond quickly to questions or comments from your audience. Through social media, you must create human and real relationships.

5) Publish constantly: Stick to an editorial calendar that provides a periodic and constant publication based on your availability.

6) Monitor the market: Try to stay up to date on changes in your target market in order to change your strategy based on new trends or needs.

7) Define evaluation metrics: What do you want to achieve with your social activity? Increase your visibility? Increase Sales? Get leads? Based on your goals, define the most

appropriate metrics for evaluating the results.

8) Monitor the results: Analyze the behavior of your audience, interactions with your social accounts, and visits to the site. Once the metrics have been defined, constantly check that the results obtained are in line with those expected and, if not, make some strategic changes.

9) Do not be in a hurry: Social Media Marketing does not provide immediate results, but it is an activity that requires competence, patience, and above all, constancy.

10) "1 is greater than 0 or is it?": Accounts not updated are a risk to the company's online reputation so if you have little time available, avoid opening a thousand different social pages and then leaving them abandoned to themselves. Alternatively, you can contact external consultants who, based on your specific needs, will be able to optimize your Social Media Marketing activity.

Chapter 1: The Importance of Social Media Marketing in 2019

For how often this is presented, the answer to the question 'is social media marketing important in 2019,' is still 'it depends'. You have to ask yourself what your goals are and once the mechanisms of advertising on Facebook are understood, the answer will be obvious to you.

If you want to intercept an audience that might be interested in your product or service, surely Facebook Ads will be for you, allowing you to submit your ads to a specific target of users.

If you have traffic on your site or e-commerce, regardless of how it is obtained, you may want to recontact those users to repropose your ads.

Do you know that when you are looking for a product

and after visiting a site, later when going to Facebook, you will find yourself the sponsored ads?

It's called *retargeting*. You will be able to create customized user lists based on their actions such as visiting a particular page (article, product, landing page, shopping cart, etc.) and exploiting them for well-targeted ads.

It will be essential to have a very clear strategy for our Facebook Ads campaign. It will be appropriate to understand where the potential customer is located within our sales funnel and submit different ads depending on whether it is far or near the purchase.

We certainly cannot offer the same ad to a potential customer who does not know our brand and someone that already has our product in his chart. This is just to say that Facebook has great potential for small businesses, but needs to be used properly to get the most out of it.

Do you really need a Social Media Marketing Plan? The answer is simple, short, direct; if you do not have a plan, you have little chance of success. Planning means making a strategy. Without a strategy in the modern market, you do not sell. Planning means selling.

But is creating a true Social Marketing Plan easy or difficult? It depends, if for you it is the first time, then you can find some difficulties. But you will see, in concrete, it is not very far from what you have already done in the past for your business. You have to reflect, compare, hypothesize, choose, understand, enhance, and finally, verify.

Using a metaphor, we could see marketing as an orchestra and the Social Marketing Plan as the score to be followed. Every marketing action is the symphony played by a single musician; the score imposes rules, times, and style. The orchestra represents the set of many instruments that play, but they play alternately with a wise strategy. Every musical instrument is important but necessary only if it follows the score. It is the conductor who decides what, when, and why.

Now, are you ready to make a Social Media

Marketing Plan? Did you understand the need? To achieve a good plan, you have to follow these 6 steps. They will simplify your life.

• Step 1: Goals — Identify the Correct Goals

The first step for any marketing strategy is to establish the goals you are hoping to achieve. The more you have clear objectives to achieve, the easier it will be to achieve them or react quickly to changes in the market and business strategies. Without a concrete objective, there is no means to measure the progress of a marketing campaign. These social goals must, of course, be aligned with the broader marketing strategy.

One of the most used methods to identify the correct objective is to pursue is the SMART approach. Smart is an acronym used to remember the 5 characteristics of the correct objective: specific (specific), measurable (measurable), attainable (attainable), pertinent (relevant), and limited in time (time-bound, with a fixed expiration).

An easy way to start your social media marketing plan is to give yourself at least two to three small goals. For example, you decide that you will share photos about the corporate culture on Instagram. You'll do this by sending 3 photos a week with the goal of getting at least 30 shares a week and 10 comments. In addition, post your short articles on Facebook (at least twice a week). This is better if related to content on your site or blog because you can directly link them and receive more visits. All activities must have a pre-established time and must be measurable and measured.

- Step 2: Market Analysis and Competition Analysis

The second step is to do a real market analysis of what can be done on every single Social Network and what your competitors are doing; obviously taking inspiration from international success stories, perhaps from your own sector.

- Step 3: Voice and Style

Each company has its own style and its own image that is usually reflected in every action; how the sales show up, the stand presented at the fair, the brochures, the business cards, the website and so on. The company cannot 'NOT communicate;' it simply does so with its headquarters and warehouse, through furniture, colors, and its logo. The actions on social must invariably communicate the style and the image that the company has strategically chosen to communicate. The marketing manager must be able to make social users perceive what the company wants them to perceive.

- Step 4: The Tools and the Channels

When you are well aware of the company style to communicate, all you need to do is identify the tools and channels you want to use. For example, LinkedIn and Facebook to create ad hoc posts on company products and services, Twitter to convey content with links to blog posts and website, Instagram to communicate photographs about corporate style, and Pinterest both to communicate style but also infographics on company services and the technologies identified.

Among the tools, we must obviously include the Web Tools that were born in recent years, dedicated to the editorial management of content on social media. Well-known tools such as Hootsuite, TweetDeck, ManageFlitter and many others, are essential for the management and analysis of social marketing.

- Step 5: Editorial Calendar, Content Plan

The fifth step gives you the opportunity to reassemble all the previous steps in a single tool, creating a real Content Plan, with precise timing divided by days, weeks, months.

The editorial calendar must reflect the objectives identified, the chosen market strategy, the company style, and the pre-established tools/channels (in the photo above, an example of a simple calendar developed in Excel).

For example, if your purpose on Instagram is to generate contacts and the one on Facebook is simply to communicate the corporate image, you must make sure that your calendar represents well these two objectives (in terms of timing, type of message, tool used, editorial consistency over time, and the number of weekly posts).

- Step 6: Constant Checking

Having implemented a Social Marketing Plan with its editorial strategy, it becomes crucial to be able to measure its progress and success, perhaps even ROI (return on investment). Also, for this step, as for the fourth, it is essential to use dedicated tools. First is Google Analytics (analysis for Blog, Website, Newsletter, Landing pages, etc.). For some time, Twitter has also been offering its Analytics for free. These and other tools allow you to analyze in detail a large amount of data grouped by type, bringing a clear picture of what works and what does not, which social leads to more visits to the website and which others are able to turn them into active contacts (customers).

Advantages and Disadvantages of Social Media Marketing

How much do Ads cost? How is the price established? It is the most frequent question in this environment, but unfortunately, there is no answer other than "it depends". On what does it depend? From what you are advertising to who your target is, how many competitors there are and what your goals are, just to mention some aspects.

Before reaching the total costs of a Facebook campaign, it is important to understand how these costs are established. Unlike traditional advertising methods, Facebook does not have a fixed price for each placement but follows a system of an auction among advertisers to get the ad published. This is because Facebook users can only see a limited number of ads per day.

There are various factors that determine which ad will be displayed, who will be shown and at what cost.

o   Who you are targeting.

As we will see later, the possibilities of targeting are many and depending on the target you choose, you will compete with other advertisers.

o   Your relevance score, engagement, and click through rate.

Facebook assigns to each ad a score of relevance from 1 to 10 depending on the associated target and its response. The higher the interaction and the number of clicks, the higher your score will be and the more likely your ad will be displayed at lower costs.

o   The timing.

The more competitive the sector is, the higher the costs will be. There will be periods of the year, such as during certain holidays where costs could increase significantly. You can choose from various options, but which one is best will depend on your campaign objectives.

You can pay in various ways:

- Per impressions: Pay for each display of your ad.
  It is better to use this option when you want to reach as many people as possible, for example, in a brand awareness campaign.

- Per click: Pay only if someone clicks on your ad.
  This option is preferable when we want to take users to click on a link that will take them to the site or to a specific landing page.

- Per action: Pay only when a user performs a certain action, how to fill out an entry form, buy a product or visit a certain page.
  With this option, most social network will show ads to people who are more likely to take one of these actions.

So, you will understand that answering the question "how much does it cost?" is complex. The important thing is to set a budget and manage it in the best way possible, reaching potential customers in a careful manner and keeping an eye on the really relevant parameters such as cost per conversion. Not knowing what you will spend is one of the main disadvantages of Facebook marketing, but still, it is something that can be overcome easily.

Chapter 2: The Most Important Channels

A lot of people that approach social media marketing for the first time think that the key is to be on every social. The truth, however, is that it is much better to focus only on the platforms that people use the most. Right now, Instagram, Facebook, and YouTube are the most used social networks, so we will focus on those three.

Instagram

Available at first only for iOS devices, in 2012, the version for Android was born, allowing a faster deployment of the application and a significant increase in the number of subscribers to the platform. It is only as a result of this great growth that Zuckerberg understands its potential, so much to decide to buy it to turn Instagram into a powerful social network, almost as long as the longest running Facebook.

According to the Instagram blog, in June 2018, registered users were 1 billion, and the data continues to grow. This makes us understand that Instagram is a social network not yet saturated and with much more to give to its users, so it proves a suitable platform for the development of new strategies of social media marketing, thanks to the use of visual storytelling with the aid of the many new features offered by the developers.

Facebook

In 2018, Facebook remains one of the main channels for marketing but, like everything in the digital world, it changes regularly and every so often. At the beginning of this year, Facebook changed the algorithm of its Newsfeed, deciding to prioritize the posts of relatives and friends (the system considers the profiles with which a user contacts more often), to those that cause discussions and conversations, and to the publication of the pages that a user has chosen to see first (See First in the preferences of the Newsfeed). Under these conditions, marketing on Facebook becomes a challenge.

YouTube

YouTube is a web-based video sharing platform set up 11 years ago by the trio Hurley, Karim, and Steve Chen. The idea of creating a social video sharing platform was particularly risky but diabolically apt.

What at the time was simply an idea, a website, in a few years has become the reference point for millions of Internet users who upload movies of any kind every day, while millions of users spend their time watching these videos every day.

The growth of YouTube has become exponential when the giant of Mountain View, Google, has decided to acquire the company and liquidate the three founders handsomely.

The commercial operation turned out to be a winner. Google, in fact, has made YouTube the third most visited website in the world, behind only the same search engine of Google to the social network par excellence Facebook.

Since YouTube has come to life and has become

what it is today, we have studied the phenomenon and our goal is to promote and give visibility to our customers also through this colossus of social media.

To date, YouTube is a hotbed of new talent, music, entertainment, and entertainment in general and is an immense advertising window for companies and individuals who have chosen the Internet as a vehicle to promote their product and their professionalism.

Chapter 3: How to Use Facebook in 2019 to Promote Your Business

The best content on Facebook in 2019 is the one that involves and stimulates communication. There is no single formula to write a successful content but there are some tricks that can help you increase the effectiveness of your posts:

- Publish posts in the best time. Analyze when your audience is online to optimize your publication time.

- Evaluate your audience. Track the performance of your posts and find out what they like most to your target and what is the winning content for your editorial plan. I will talk shortly about the importance of analytics.

- Take advantage of current issues and trends. Find out what are the topics that infect users using services like Google Trends, Trending Topic on social media, or follow the calendar of events for your industry (even local ones if they are relevant to you).

- Use the questions as a call-to-action to encourage users to leave comments under your own publication.

- Miscellaneous content. The predictability of your posts can damage your strategy. Try different types of content, alternating topics and formats of your publications to not bore your audience.

The video format is interesting not only because Facebook tends to prioritize it, but also because, among the various types of content that you can publish on your page, it is the one most loved by users.

Here is a small selection of tips for video optimization for Facebook:

o Upload videos directly to Facebook because posts with YouTube links lose visibility (Facebook gives priority to videos uploaded on its platform).

o Ideal format: Facebook recommends using MP4 and MOV, a complete list of recommended formats you can find. Facebook recommends uploading videos with a maximum duration of 15 seconds with an attractive and high-quality content.

o The public on Facebook also appreciates longread texts when they are written well (if the theme is current, it is easy to generate conversions). Why shouldn't the same rule work for the video?

o Upload the videos with subtitles (about 85% of videos is shown without the sound) and do not forget to add a title and a small description to make people understand the subject of the video right away.

o Video streaming is another type of content that Facebook likes so much and can get yourself a good organic reach. When you create a Live on Facebook, all your friends and followers will be notified of the start of a new stream, so everyone can follow and comment on your video live.

Content marketing and content curation are two of the words that most marketers will be interested in this year. Content marketing is a much more extensive approach that is not limited to the Facebook channel but can play a decisive role on the same platform. I speak of the choice and creation of content to be conveyed in their fan page that. If chosen accurately, with an attractive graphics and communicated in the right way (sometimes even in the right time), it can become "viral," and is going to end even outside of our primary user target. However, by doing so, it could give us the advantage of expanding our brand positioning to other target users, who until then, were thought to be uninterested in us. Translated into simple words; the content conveyed on the page, through sharing and "like", can attract new users to know our brand and start to follow it from the page.

Facebook insights provide much more data than before, and the service is almost similar to Google Analytics. Periodically "combing" the data helps to better understand what are the content most appreciated by users and those that generate greater shares (now we can also know what are the comments with negative "sentiment", even if the service is not very reliable). From the analysis of our pages and those of our customers, it appears that quality images (especially those released for the first time and then created in-house) and videos (in second place) are those that reach the best level of engagement (likes, shares, comments) and consequently are more likely to spread our brand/product making it known to new users.

Once you get to the advanced level, it is important to start outsourcing your advertising campaigns so that you can focus on other parts of the business. In particular, it is fundamental to outsource the client profiling process. Here are some interesting instruction that can help you speed up the process.

To define the profile of your ideal customer, you have to remember that each individual is influenced by his position in society. Therefore, to trace the profile of the ideal customer, we must answer questions related to these influences.

Social Influences

Cultural Systems and Subsystems

- How old is he?
- Where does he live?
- Is he a man, a woman, or both?
- What degree of education does he/she have? What schools did he/she attend?
- What hobbies or passions do they have?
- What are its values?
- What are their beliefs?

Social Class

- What kind of work do they do?

- How much does he or she earn?

Family

- Is he or she married?
- Does he or she have children? How many?
- Does he live alone and is single?
- Does he live by his parents?

Marketing Influences

- Do they already use a product to meet the need or solve the problem?
- What kind of product do they use?
- What kind of brand?
- What features are relevant?
- What is the benefit most appreciated?
- On what price range is it oriented?
- Is the high price for the customer a way of affirming their social status?
- Do they associate high price with quality?
- What kind of advertising influences their purchase?
- Where do they usually buy?

Situational Influences

- Which environments can influence the purchase (showroom, the point of sale)?

Social Environment

- Within the group in which he/she lives and works, who else influences the choice of purchase?
- Who uses the product?
- Who pays for the product?
- Are the influencer, the consumer, and the buyer the same person?

Psychological Aspects Associated with the Product

- What are their fears?
- What problems do they want to solve?
- What consequences would it entail for an unsolved problem?
- What are the challenges they're facing?
- What are their wishes?

Emotional Aspects Related to the Choice of the Product

- What mistakes are they afraid to commit by making a wrong choice?
- What would it mean for the customer to choose a wrong product?

Now that you have answered these questions, you can trace the profile of the ideal customer. Here's how to proceed.

Put a face to your potential client (download a photo from the internet that identifies the physical characteristics of your potential customer) and a fictitious name. Then compile the data that will trace the characteristics of socio-demographic, psycho-graphic, and consumer experiences. This serves to have a clear representation of him/her with whom we are going to talk and with whom we want to relate.

This exercise can lead to a great transformation to your company. In fact, it will help you understand the motivating beliefs, fears, and secret desires that influence the purchase decisions of the customer and tunes your marketing efforts and understand what solutions to offer to your market.

A great resource to boost this process and find people that met your avatar standards on Facebook is lookup-id.com. Thanks to this website, you can define your target customer through the definition of personal characteristics and get a list of people that met them. Here is how it works.

Once that you have entered the website, go on the "extract members" section. It is very easy to find on the top right of the page. From there, you want to insert the ID of a Facebook in your niche, which of course will contain people in the target with your offer. The website will give you a complete and detailed list of the people in the group, which means that you have just discovered a goldmine since those will be on the target for what you are offering.

On this website, you can even use the FB Search function. Once you have designed the features of your typical prospect, you can insert them in this platform to get a list of users that meet those standards. It is pretty straightforward and it is very easy to use. Our suggestion is to play around with the website and get a grasp of its potential. Once you start using it, you will never get back at the classic manual research.

Now, it is time to use another great tool to make life easier and start gathering a following. First, install Toolkit for Facebook by PlugEx. What is this? It is an amazing tool that will allow you to do multiple actions in a matter of seconds. For instance, once you have your list and have launched Toolkit by PlugEx, you can then invite all those people to put a like on your page or to join your group.

When you start using these tools on a regular basis, you will be amazed at how easy it is to grow your fan base and start getting significant results. One little tip that we like to give our readers is to always use a secondary account for these operations in order to guarantee proper privacy protection.

A Practical Example

Now that we have seen how to use the two software in theory, it is time to dive into the practice and use a practical example to understand the concepts better.

So, let's say that we have a shop that sells running gear and we want to find customers that are on the target with the items we sell. The first thing we want to do is to go on running groups, like this one, **https://www.facebook.com/groups/TrailAndUltraRunning/** and look for the group id. We can do that by going here, **https://lookup-id.com/** and entering the previous URL. This will give us the ID of the group. After that, we just need to paste the group ID here, **https://lookup-id.com/get_facebookid.php** to get a list of all the members that are inside the group.

After having done that, you can use Toolkit for Facebook by PlugEx to quickly invite all the people on the list you just found to leave a like on your dedicated running store page. Furthermore, you can even invite them to your very own group where you will start your marketing process.

This is how you can use the two software together to really boost up your experience. Another great thing you can outsource is the retargeting phase. Once you have acquired a potential client, you can use an automated bot to close the sale for you. Here are some suggestions we found very valuable.

If you're not using ManyChat, right now you're losing 60% of new potential customers. (You're literally burning your money!)

Does this seem absurd?

Perhaps you do not know that the Chatbots are the future of marketing. Soon, we will see together what they are. For now, know that they have incredible power; to enter people's lives like never before.

Of course, there are e-mails, but, think about it. Would anyone really open a promotional e-mail? The truth is that some, when they find them in the mailbox, they almost automatically discard them. They have developed a natural tendency to delete promotional emails. They associate the email with invasive advertising on at work or, again, at the studio. To talk to a friend, however, they use WhatsApp or Facebook Messenger.

What Do We Want to Say?

You should choose the tool to use based on your audience. For example, it is made up of managers who often check e-mails, then e-mail marketing may be the ideal choice. On the other hand, if you turn to students, on average 20 years, and who have much more convenience with the chat; it would be better to think of a Facebook Bot.

Do you understand what the extraordinary advantage is? It will allow you to establish an authentic communication with your (potential or not) customer who will open your message just like a friend. You will receive a notification on your mobile phone, you can chat with them; everything automatically.

The only thing you will have to deal with is the Bot settings. The good news is that it is an extremely simple operation. Thanks to the services available, you will use more or less 10 minutes. However, without knowing how to use this very powerful tool effectively, you would risk undermining this work. Therefore, in this chapter, we will introduce you to the correct configuration of a Chatbot with ManyChat.

Are you ready? Let's start!

What Is ManyChat and Create a Facebook Bot in 10 Minutes

We can say that a Bot is a program that is able to manage, in an automatic and natural way, conversations in a chat with users. It can answer questions, offer solutions to problems and make proposals, just as if it were human.

Already from this general definition, you will have guessed that you have in your hands something potentially revolutionary for you and your business. You will free your time, increasing your results.

ManyChat, What Is It?

In short, it is the simplest and most intuitive service to create a Facebook Messenger Bot. You do not need programming knowledge. The configuration is extremely fast, and you will immediately have the opportunity to carry out a series of actions:

- Create automated message sequences.
- Send a message to all users registered in the bot.
- Use advanced tools to increase conversions.

How ManyChat Works: The 2 Basic Tools for Bot Marketing

We have just said that ManyChat is the easiest to use Messenger Marketing tool. Despite its simplicity, however, it offers several features that make it complete and effective for your web marketing strategy. Do you want some examples?

- Automatic sequences.

This is the series of messages that, automatically, ManyChat will send to the user. You can set them as you like, based on your lead generation strategy.

- Growth Tools.

Here, this is the real bomb among the tools offered. They are a series of "extensions" that add functionality to ManyChat. The most famous is Facebook Comments Tool, which allows you to convert whoever who comments on a particular post into a member of the Bot. (These are just some of the features you'll have available.)

Well, to make you better understand the functioning of a Chatbot, let's assume a case of real use.

The user, Luke, comments on the post of your product with the specific keyword that you have set. Your bot turns on and automatically sends your opt-in message; basically, a welcome message to confirm the user's interest. Subsequently, based on the behavior of Luke, the bot will send him different messages to achieve the goals you have set. These messages are part of an "automated sequence" that you created earlier.

The important thing is to never be intrusive. Keep this in mind during the setup phase. Each time you send a message, a notification will be sent to Luke's mobile phone. This means two things:

- You will enter in his daily life;
- You will have to manage this opportunity in the best way, so as not to frustrate him (most people are not accustomed to this tool just yet, so do not overuse it).

Chapter 4: Facebook and Organic Promotion

Small and medium-sized businesses can use Facebook marketing strategies with high margins of success. In fact, with more than 2 billion active users every month, it is impossible to remove the blue social from your web marketing plan.

What Could Be the Goals of Facebook Marketing Referring to SMEs?

Brand Awareness

Facebook is a very important tool that enables small and medium-sized enterprises (SMEs) to make their products and services known while at the same time cultivating a very direct relationship with interested users.

If on the one hand your community, made up of people who already know your products, can follow us on the blue social; on the other side, it is possible to reach people who do not know us through spontaneous sharing, or through sponsored ones. The latter, through the creation of the right audience, allow reaching to new people potentially interested in our products.

Customer Care

Facebook is also one of the websites that best lend themselves to customer care, which is assistance to its customers. Indeed, given the announcement of future updates of the algorithm of the views of the Newsfeed, focus on customer care could also prove successful in terms of awarding the content posted.

Promotional content can still be valid but using your own social page as a place to solve problems and perplexities of its users can be a key to use highly because it is able to trigger conversations between friends, debates, and an engagement appreciated by Facebook algorithms.

Direct Sales

Facebook can also be used to sell your products or services. Like an e-commerce site, the platform lends itself to the possibility of direct purchase from the page, with huge benefits for users. For small and medium-sized businesses, this opportunity is an important resource for saving resources that would otherwise have to be spent on the creation and management of an entire site.

Obviously, it must be said that those who hold an important business cannot simply rely on the social network of Zuckerberg to market their products online, but it is a fact that not a month passes in which the Menlo Park team does not make availability of some new function that favors those who want to sell via the web.

How to Create a Facebook Marketing Strategy That Works?

Before starting to take action on Facebook, it is good for small and medium-sized businesses to devote time to creating a well-designed communication plan.

First, the goals of the strategies to be put in place must be defined. Secondly, the public must be identified; that is the buyer, the typical customer, tracing a sort of identikit of its main characteristics such as age, place of residence, interests, level of education and more (see chapter 6 for more information about this topic). As for the content, it will be good to dedicate only 20% of them to the promotion of your products or services so as not to tire the user with continuous offers and hype.

Finally, the tools for checking the results must not be forgotten, with the choice of the most appropriate metrics to follow in order to understand the effectiveness of the steps taken along the road to achieving the designated objectives. For example, if the setting up of a valid customer care campaign has been done, one of the ways to evaluate the effectiveness of the actions carried out is the analysis of the number and quality of comments received, rather than that of 'likes'.

Facebook for Small Businesses

Why should you use Facebook to market your small business?

Facebook is about to touch the ceiling of a billion users according to the latest official data released in July. The people who connect to this social network are 955 every month and 552 million every day; more than half a billion, even the number of monthly users who connect to Facebook with a mobile device — mobile phone, smartphone, and tablet.

Facebook is becoming, for many, a major source of information more and more often, instead of connecting to the homepage of newspapers to see what is happening. We scroll the dashboard reading and commenting on the news linked by our friends. The 2011 CENSIS report on the American company shows that Facebook is used as a source of information by 26.8% of Americans, a percentage that grows to 61.5% in the age group of 14 to 29 years.

The quantity and nature of our relationships have been radically changed by the possibility of keeping in touch with people we do not see daily in person, but for the most diverse circumstances, we feel close. They were our friends in the past, we shared a travel experience or study, or we met online and subsequently met live.

This allows us to listen and exchange opinions, information, points of view, and emotions in this impetuous dynamic of conversations. This is an always open bar where people pass from one group to another participating in dozens of discussions. The companies suddenly find themselves "degraded" to one voice among others, which must gain attention thanks to the importance of what it says without the possibility of massively occupying the spaces of visibility. Furthermore, we must learn to speak "with" people, which mean, first of all, to listen and respond.

Should your company, association, electoral committee, theatre company, or excitement have a presence on Facebook? In the vast majority of cases, the answer is yes. Do not fall into the trap of thinking that Facebook is exclusively the realm of lazy people; often, it is a great way to "feel the pulse" of your stakeholders and can intercept your needs and opportunities that otherwise you would not have known.

In addition to your site where people go once in a while, or maybe they never go back; on the contrary, many of them open Facebook every day, several times a day. If they find what you publish to be interesting enough for them to click on "like" or leave a comment, this makes you visible on the bulletin board of their friends, not in the anonymous way of a flyer tucked in the mailbox, but with the social support of word of mouth.

An effective presence on Facebook can help you:

- Increase your visibility, spreading the posts of your blog, the videos you shoot, and the photos you take.
- Establish a more intense relationship with your customers, better knowing their needs, and obtaining important feedback on what you do.
- Motivate and gratify your "super fans".
- Promote and share initiatives, special offers, and new products.

A Facebook group is a micro-community within the largest community of the network that, focusing on specific themes, attracts people to the target. To this, we add that the groups have recently had the blessing of Facebook after the hard blow to the business pages in the latest updates of the EdgeRank algorithm.

What happened to the Facebook algorithm?

The turning point came with the announcement of Zuckerberg and the subsequent official confirmation on the blog of Facebook news. In fact, the Newsroom informs users of an epochal change — less visibility on the pages in favor of a more personal communication. More visibility for the posts of friends and family; but also explicitly mentioned by Zuckerberg, to the groups. Unlike pages, in fact, groups have a greater predisposition to the generation of discussions and not to the simple unilateral posting of content. Precisely, this content with little interaction is the one against which Facebook wants to fight. The decision comes after the progressive descent of the engagement on the posts that are, over the years, has characterized the Social Network of Menlo Park.

What does this mean?

It simply means that the posts on the groups will have greater visibility and the possibility to reach more easily your target audience. It seems to me, therefore, an excellent idea not to neglect them.

How to Find Facebook Groups in Target

Let us imagine, of course, that you have already identified the niche or sector on which to base your communication strategy. The first of the problems you need to solve is to find groups to distribute your content on. I'll show you a couple of techniques you can use.

1) Facebook Searches

If you have an active Facebook account in America, you can use the search bar to find groups that meet your requirements. For example, if you look for a group that deals with social, you can write "social media" on the search bar and then apply the filter "groups" (Facebook will initially search among posts, people, and so on).

If you want to get even smarter, I recommend you to use Facebook in English. You will open other very interesting possibilities! Facebook in English supports the "Graph Search", thanks to which it is possible to create more complex searches such as "Groups joined by my friends who like social media". That is, look for groups to which were added by part of my friends who like social media.

Or you might still be looking for users who like certain pages or groups in an area of interest. For example, "Friends who like Wired". You can then go to peek at the groups in which your friends have entered, going directly to their profile (privacy permitting!).

2) Use Facebook Tips
One thing we can be extremely sure of is that Facebook knows us more than we think. It is for this reason that it will be easy for them to suggest

groups that might be interesting to you based on the past history of your likes and the groups in which you are already inside.

Just go to the Facebook page dedicated to groups. On the upper part of the drop-down menu, you can enter the "Discover" tab. Here you will find lots of suggestions divided by categories including the "local" one to find geographically close groups. This feature is available on both desktop and mobile. In the latter case, you will go to the main menu> Groups> Suggested.

I'll remind you that the specific features of the groups were recently incorporated into the main app of Facebook, while the app "Facebook Groups" retired in September 2017.

What to Do Before Posting Content in Groups

I already know that you're cheating to publish your content on the groups of your interest, but before starting to spam, I'll suggest that you follow some rules.

1) Always look carefully at group usage policies.

Any self-respecting group manager sets up rules in their own group to prevent the occurrence of phenomena such as SPAM, excesses of OT (Off Topic, i.e. ending off the arguments to which the group is dedicated), too much promotion, trolling, and so on.

This means that there may be rules on the amount of content that can be submitted to the community, for example. Or that you can publish external links to Facebook only with the permission of the admin.

Policies are often indicated in the first post above, often attached with a "pin". Or they could be in the "file" section of the group. Study these rules well and behave accordingly.

2) Keep to general rules of good behavior.

Apart from the policies which rightly dictate contents, times and rhythms, there are also rules of good common life that should always be respected. If you produce content in large quantities:

- Do not spam it all the time.
- Always check that it is in theme with the group, that they are of quality, and that they can be useful and relevant.
- If possible, add a note to the article, a textual status that (for example) highlights a sentence of the article or that poses a question capable of generating a valuable discussion.

Remember, these are not only your contents! Subscribe to the groups, be in silent mode, and then spam your news as if there is no tomorrow. These will certainly irritate the admin that at some point, they might even think to kick you out! Even more so later in this historical moment in which the use of statistics of the group has been made available to the administrators.

My advice is to always balance your content with content from other sources. And it would be desirable to participate in the discussions, in addition to the normal posting! If you already produce your content and think that it is sufficient for your strategy, it means that you skipped the previous paragraph. Go read it!

For a content strategy, whether linked to the development of your business or to your personal branding, you need news and content about your industry. I know I'm repetitive, but I'll write it again; you cannot just talk about yourself! To find valid content on the web, you can use many tools like the simplest monitoring software (think of Google Alerts or Talkwalker) or news aggregator sites like Feedly.

In the era of the so-called "content shock", where our ability to absorb information is definitely lower than the amount of content produced, the figure of the creator becomes of primary importance. Skimming the contents and proposing the best to a community, therefore, becomes a primary role.

Additional Tips

Create a Network for Your Loyal Fans

This group is made up of the most loyal fans, people who believe in your company, in your product, and in your values. Brands like Canva, who has a loyal fan base, called these groups "community groups" or "ambassador groups".

The one with the loyal fans is the most important group you can create on Facebook. It is important to create a positive word of mouth on your products, your company, and your activities. Be sure to make your fans feel special. You can do it in various ways; by sending a shirt or by putting a comment on them.

The most important thing is to thank them, heartily and regularly. A written note (maybe by hand), is much more pleasant than a gift. Thank your fans for helping you grow your community and achieve your goals. Here are 5 ways you can use these groups:

1) Get feedback on new products.

You have a new product to launch but first, you want to know how it would be accepted? This is the right place to test it.

2) Attract new members.

If your company has a membership program, this is a great way to keep in touch with them and attract new ones.

3) Answer the questions.

How many times have you seen a question on a group or an online forum and you have thought that your product could be the ideal solution? Of course, you could answer the question with your private profile, but you will be more successful by responding to the members of your group.

Answer often to questions and to avoid spam (especially if there are many members in the group), tag two or three experts in the response that can respond appropriately.

4) Recruit experts.

Many people like to feel expert and be taken into consideration. And many like to share their knowledge with other people. Experienced people can help new consumers get closer to your product and buy it. Please note that it may be necessary to create a dedicated expert group.

5) Share the company's achievements.

If the company wins a prize or is named in an important publication, let the whole world know about it. You can then call your friends, family, post the news on your private profile, but in this way, you will not go very far. If your company receives a prize, share the news with the fan group. That is why Facebook exists.

Help Your Customers

The second type of Facebook groups is dedicated to acquired customers. To build this community, invite people to join the group as soon as they make a purchase. Make customers aware of the existence of the group and that you would like them if they too registered.

Explain how the group works in the "information" section, as Golden Tote does. For example, members can get to know each other, share ideas and strategies, and help each other in any way.

Be sure to send an email with the link to subscribe to the group and monitor who signs up or not. Do not forget to invite people who have not yet registered several times.

Ways to develop your group on Facebook:

- Be generous and promote a "give" policy.
  For example, offer tips or tricks to use the less known features of your product and invite other users to share their findings. You could invite members of your fan group to share tips and tricks with them too.

- Be transparent.
  Respond personally to customer criticism. For example, acknowledge the customer who makes you notice what is lacking in your product and respond that you will immediately fix it.

It is not necessary to promise discounts or promotions to the disgruntled customer, but it is important to thank him for the report, to apologize and to promise that he will be contacted when the problem is solved.

- Be present.
  Answer questions and comments as soon as possible. If you cannot give an immediate answer, still let your customer know that you will respond quickly. From suggestions, tips, tricks, encourage other users to share their findings.

- Be inclusive.
  Offer group members promotions and offers that are not on the official page. Make your customers feel part of an exclusive club. If a social media user shows a particular interest in your product, he also invites you to join the online group.

Grow Target Segments (With Multiple Facebook Groups)

One of the most important goals of marketers is to develop a "typical customer", that is to identify their customers and understand their doubts, problems, and how your product can meet its needs.

If you have different types of customers, create more groups on Facebook. For example, you could create a group based on the language spoken by its users. Maybe not all customers will want to be considered experts and to answer questions from other users, you can then create smaller groups to meet the needs of each client.

Now that we have seen how Facebook groups can have a profound impact on your social media marketing strategy, it is time to see how to create your very own group. Managing your own Facebook group may seem complicated at first but will pay off quite a lot in the long run.

Maybe you do not know, but creating a group on Facebook allows you to share photos, videos, and anything else just with whoever you want. Thanks to groups, you can interact with a small circle of people without the others seeing what you're sharing with them.

Even if you do not consider yourself a social network expert, you can feel comfortable. In the next paragraphs, you will find all the information you need to create a Facebook group, whether you intend to act on your PC or your mobile device. In addition, you can find some useful tips for creating group chats on Messenger and use them to share various types of information with friends and relatives. What do you say? Are you ready to start? So let's put aside the talk and get straight into the heart of this tutorial. I wish you good reading and have fun!

Wanting to create a group on Facebook but unfamiliar with the social network founded by Mark Zuckerberg, you do not have the faintest idea how to proceed? No fear! Just follow the steps listed below to complete the task.

PC

To create a group on Facebook, from your PC, connect by the browser to the website of the social network (Of course, after you have already logged-in to your account.) and click on the green Create Group button located at the top right.

In the box that opens, type the name you want to assign to the group in the text field located under the entry 'give a name to the group', select the users you want to include in the latter by typing their names or their email addresses in the field text placed under the entry 'add some people' and then select one of the privacy settings available to decide who will be able to view the content posted. Select 'public group' to allow all users of Facebook to view the group and the content posted in it; 'group closed' to allow everyone to find the group and see the members but without being able to view the posts or 'secret group' to allow only members of the group to find it and view its posts.

After choosing the name of the group, the members that will be part of it and the privacy settings, click on the blue button 'create', select an icon that identifies the latter (e.g. the icon of the basketball, if your new group is dedicated to the world of basketball or the camera icon, if your group talks about photography) and click on the blue 'OK button'. If you wish, you can also skip this step by clicking on the 'skip' button.

Once the procedure is complete, you will be sent back to the main page of your group, which you can customize by inserting a cover image. To do so, click on the green 'upload photo' button and upload an image saved on your PC, or click on the 'select photos' button to use an image from those you have already uploaded to your Facebook profile.

To interact with friends who are part of the group, click on 'post to write a new post', click on the item 'add photo/video' to insert a multimedia content or on the voice 'live video' to start a live broadcast with other members of the group.

After creating the group, click on the options that are located immediately below the name of the group (top left); "Information", to add a description to the group;

"Discussion", to share content with other members; "Members", to view members who are part of the group and to modify their roles; "Events", to create an event on the group or "Manage the group", to create scheduled posts, accept subscription requests, view the activities of administrators and so on.

To change other settings concerning the new Facebook group you have created, click the 'more' button (after clicking on the 'discussion' option) and, in the menu that appears, click on one of the options you see; "Add members", to add new members to the group or "Edit group settings", to change their name, select the group type (that is, the category related to the topic dealt with in the same), link a page, select who can publish a post and so on.

Android

To create a group on Facebook from your Android device, first, start the official social network app on your smartphone or tablet and log in to your account (if required). Then tap on the symbol (≡) located at the top right, press the 'create group' button (located under the heading Groups), type the name of the group in the text field 'give a name to this group' and, if you wish, press on the camera symbol to take or add a photo.

Then add the members to be included in the group by selecting them from the menu located at the bottom of the screen and press the 'next' button. At this point, select the privacy settings by ticking one of the available options; "Public", to create a public group and then allow anyone to view the posts and members that are part of it; "Closed", to hide the posts published on the group to those who are not members or "Private", to make the group "invisible" to those who are not part of it. After indicating the privacy options you prefer the most, press on the item 'create'. Et voilà! You've just created your group on Facebook!

Even on Android, you can add new members, edit group info, create events, post photos, files and anything else using the appropriate commands that you find immediately under the name that identifies the group.

iOS

To create a group on Facebook from your iOS device, start the Facebook application, log in to your account (if necessary), press the symbol (≡) located at the bottom right and then tap on the item "Groups". In the screen that opens, press the symbol (+) located at the top right, type the name of the group in the text field "Give a name to this group" and, if you wish, press the symbol of the camera to shoot or add a photo to be used as a cover for the group.

Now, choose the members to add to the group by selecting them from the menu at the bottom and press the 'next' button. Then select the privacy settings by ticking one of the available options; "Public", to create a public group; "Closed", to hide the posts published on the group to those who are not part of it or "Private", to not allow those who are not members of the group to find it, nor to display the posts. Finally, press the item "Create" to complete the group creation procedure.

Now you can finally customize your new group, add new members, edit the info, post photos and anything else using the buttons that are immediately below the name and photo of the group itself.

Create a Chat Group Along with Your Group

If your intention is simply to converse with other Facebook users, you probably do not need to create real Facebook groups, but you can simply create simple group chats using the appropriate feature included in Messenger.

- To create a group chat on PC, log in to your Facebook account from the browser, click on the "Messenger" icon (the lightning bolt symbol at the top), click on the item "New group", type the name of the group chat in the text field "Assign a name to the group", select the users to add to the chat and click the blue "Create" button.

- To create a group chat on smartphones and tablets, however, start the Messenger app on your device, press on the voice "Groups", tap on the item "New group" (on Android) or

"Create" (on iOS) and finally press on 'arrow symbol' (on Android) or on the "Create group entry" (on iOS) to complete the operation.

When discussing Social Media as an engine for the growth of an online business and specifically Facebook Marketing, we tend to think about Fan Pages and how to exploit them to make brand awareness and generate web traffic.

In reality, on Facebook, there is another very powerful tool and in some cases even more effective than the fan pages. We are talking about Facebook Groups. Although it may seem a lot less "cool", a successful Facebook group can be a very interesting channel for acquiring web traffic.

In this chapter, we will discuss some very useful tips to quickly grow a Facebook group.
Before entering into the heart of this topic, I would like to make a small premise. As you may already know, a new business begins to achieve extraordinary results when it manages to create around itself a community of similar people with shared interests. By dealing

with digital projects, our focus will be moving towards a specific type of community; the online community, the concept that is right behind a Facebook group.

Anatomy of an Online Community

Generally, an online community consists of three distinct categories of users:

- 90% are lurkers in public.
- 9% is the average contributors.
- 1% is loyalists.

By lurker, we mean all those users, who hide among the members of a community, and who observe, read and use the information shared by the group, but without then going to interact and feed the conversation.

Why do they behave this way? Maybe because they believe they are not up to certain discussions, perhaps because they are shy people even in digital, or because an active participation still entails a waste of energy and time to devote to the online conversation. Then there is the average contributor, those who together make up 9% of the community, and who share useful contents from time to time, with a variable frequency.

Lastly, there is the hardcore of the online community, 1% of the "Highlander", or rather the loyalists. They are the ones who check every day the postings spread in the group, ask questions, provide feedback to other users, and that would continue to feed the conversation in the group if it were not that at some point of the day you still have to eat and sleep!

Why Should We Focus on the Online Community of a Facebook Group?

One of the greatest benefits of developing a community on Facebook is the concept of target reach. It is well known that a post published on a Facebook page organically reaches only a very small part of the fans of that page while, if you post the same content on a Facebook group, such sharing will be notified to every single member of the community. So the coverage of a post is far higher within a Facebook group and therefore also all actions related to it. It is a very useful tool to generate web traffic for a company or personal site. However, to be really effective, it must be based on interesting metrics. There's that factor of the number of participating members too. I would, therefore, like to share some very useful tips to quickly grow the user base of a successful Facebook group.

- Perform a preliminary analysis.

First, you need to ask yourself what the topics are and these will be the subject of discussion of the group you want to develop. As a result, you will be able to outline a profile of your ideal target. You cannot aim to have anyone enrolled in your Facebook community; you have to aim for the right people.

Ask yourself what your group is about. This will also be the answer concerning who really is your ideal target and what are its main characteristics. For more profiling, you can always make sure that the members themselves define themselves better. Create market research in which you try to extrapolate more or less information about the people themselves.

- Set goals.

Once you have a clear idea of the context on which your group revolves, it's time to think about what goal you want to pursue thanks to the Facebook group. Do you do it for personal interests than for your brand? Why do you like networking with professionals like you? Or why do you simply want to create a community of people available to each other?

Whatever your goal, having defined it will help you adapt each situation to pursue the search results.

- Set it up the right way.

A successful Facebook group cannot ignore, first of all, an effective name, which is as simple as it is attractive, and which can arouse curiosity and interest. Also, think about any keywords that may be useful for searches on the internal Facebook engine.

About keywords, on the sidebar of a Facebook group or in the general settings (which you can access by clicking on the three points on the top right, near the cover image), you find a field where you can define up to 3 tags, useful for being able to be found by people.

For proper setup, take into consideration the clear description that explains what topics are treated in the group and what kind of people are registered. In addition, you will also have to decide whether to set the group as closed, public, or secret.

Starting from the last just mentioned, a secret group can be found on Facebook only by its members while a public group allows anyone, even those who are not part of the community, to see the posts shared within it.

The most effective type to quickly acquire new members in the Facebook group is the closed one. A closed group can be found by any user during a search on Facebook using the appropriate keywords but only members can see the content published in it. Therefore, those who are really interested in consulting what is within the group must first register. This could be an interesting profiling process though, so think about it before deciding whether to create a public or secret group.

- Define the rules.

A healthy relationship, even the virtual one, between people must be based on clear and precise rules. Without the guidelines, anarchy would reign and anyone could do what they like. For example, you could only share links related to your site, constantly spamming, and you could respond in the comments using unpolished tones. This could cause serious damage to the image of the group which is difficult to repair in a short time. In addition to this set of rules, which in digital jargon is called netiquette, you must also know how to handle cases in which heated discussions are developed between the various members.

We must, therefore, intervene, bring order and try to make sure that members can return to converse with calm tones. It is the so-called crisis management. If, in the case, certain unpleasant situations persist, such as the continuous sharing of posts related to personal services, these articles should be removed. The responsible person should be warned and possibly banned, should he repeat this behavior several times.

- Share useful content.

Doing Content Marketing is essential everywhere on the web, let alone in a successful Facebook group. If you do not share valuable content, you do not feed the discussion among the members, and in that absence, there are no reasons for having to be part of an online community. So, it is essential to design an editorial plan for your Facebook group, both in terms of content creation (creation of original content) and content curation (sharing of useful material created by other people). In addition, if you want to optimize your work, you can always use one of the various digital tools available for post-programming on a Facebook group. For example, you could try PostPickr; it is a very useful tool that can help you take your business to the next level.

To increase the acquisition of new members and

above all increase the engagement of those already present, as the group's admin, you have to publish with a certain regularity, perhaps even including questions in the texts of the posts to fuel a constructive debate between the people. It could be once a day, twice a day, or even less, such as 2-3 times a week.

The important thing is that you understand one thing; you have to offer quality content that can really arouse interest and be useful to your subscribers.

Also, remember two other interesting features of Facebook groups:

- You can highlight a post compared to the others (the "Pin the post" feature). For example, if you find that a content can prove to be of absolute value for all members or if you want to keep the rules of the community easy to consult.

- In addition to publishing links, you can also upload files (for example, a pdf file), conduct surveys, direct live events, organize events and create documents linked to the group.

- Shape your team.

In the beginning, when the group consists of a few tens or hundreds of members, it will not be necessary to have other collaborators to manage the community. However, when you start having thousands of participants, the situation could get out of hand; too many requests for registration links sharing of dubious usefulness, colored verbal exchanges between members, etc. A simple remedy is to ask for help from other people, in short, set up a team of admin and moderators of the group. Both these figures can:

- Approve or deny access to the group.
- Approve or deny the publication of a post.
- Remove posts and comments.
- Remove and ban members.
- Highlight a post.

The substantial difference that exists between an administrator of a group and a moderator is that the former can offer and remove the role of admin or moderator to other members, and can make changes to the general settings of the group (name, cover photo, privacy level, etc.).

- Promote the group.

If your tactics for organic and natural growth are tight and you want to take advantage of other techniques to quickly increase the number of members of your community, I suggest you try the following strategies.

First of all, you could start Facebook advertising campaigns to reach new people potentially interested in your group. The Facebook Ads do not allow you to create a post natively sponsored for the promotion of a group but there is a simple trick to turn the obstacle. So what you can do is create a Facebook page related to your group, create an advertisement linked to it and enter the URL address of your Facebook group in the field associated with the website to be sponsored. In this way, people will be conveyed directly to your online community and, if they are really interested in the topics you have proposed, they will not hesitate to register.

Another possibility to increase the number of members is represented by cross-promotions. It is about making new collaborations with other Facebook groups more or less related to the issues faced by your community. The purpose of this collaboration is based on the exchange of promotions between groups. Just publish the URL address of the partner group and invite their members to follow the other group, if they consider it appropriate.

Chapter 5: Facebook and paid advertising

AdWords vs. Facebook

This is a question that people that are not experienced marketers often ask. The answer is always "it depends". We need to understand what the goals are that we want to achieve with our advertising campaign. It is often fundamental to combine both strategies. It all depends on the type of question; whether this is latent or conscious (or both). If the goal is to make branding and then stimulate users who do not know us and may be interested (latent demand), then the best choice is Facebook Ads which will allow you, as we will see later, to reach potential customers. You can do this with various types of targeted campaigns and get leads.

Similarly, you can also take advantage of ads on the Google Display Network to reach potential customers by submitting your banners to specific placements. If users are already looking for your product or service, the right approach is to use Google AdWords by creating ads on the Search Network. In this case, the user is already in a much lower part of the funnel, therefore more inclined to purchase as he is looking for your product/service. Obviously, in most cases, we will find both types of demand and we will have to work on both platforms jointly. The key thing is to understand where the user is inside our sales funnel and act accordingly; we will never tire of stressing it.

Going inside, it will be useful to retarget users who have shown interest in the product or service working with both Facebook Ads and AdWords through ads on the display network.

Attention; what if we intercept potential customers on Facebook through FB Ads and these then look for us on Google but we are not positioned in an organic way (without paying) for that keyword?

Simple, they will click on a competition link. The risk is, therefore, to practically advertise competitors. Understand well then how important it is, in the absence of organic positioning with SEO, that we must also have Google ads on the search network to cover some keywords as well.

The fact is that Facebook marketing is not so powerful if done alone. It is something that some people see as a disadvantage.

Each Facebook campaign consists of 3 levels and it starts from the campaign level, which consists of one or more ad groups. As you have just read, for each campaign you create, you will have to choose a goal. This is the real distinctive factor at the campaign level.

At the Ad Group level (Ad Set), you will have to choose the target, the available budget, the publication times, the offer and the placements (placements). Going down the hierarchy, at the level of the announcements, you can set the type of announcement (image, video, carousel, etc.), all the texts, the call to action (action button) and the destination links. As mentioned, the structure is hierarchical, so if you pause (or delete) for example a group of ads, the same thing will happen to all ads below that group.

The Definition of the Goals

Now that we understand the structure of a Facebook campaign and what are the parameters to be set for each level, we are ready to launch our first campaign. The first question is "What is the goal to be achieved?" Do you want to sell a certain product because maybe you have an e-commerce store, want to create awareness, or reputation, or do you want to have leads or what?

Often, in a complete web marketing strategy, we will have to create different campaigns for the different phases of the purchasing process. We can then create different ads depending on whether the target user does not know our brand or knows it but does not know our product/service, or for example, knows our product/service and may be interested in a commercial offer.

Facebook itself, in the creation phase, will propose you with different objectives divided into 4 macro-categories. Let's see them in detail one by one.

Brand Awareness

When to use it: In large-scale campaigns, when there is not a particular action that you want to take to the user. This goal will be more attractive to large companies that can afford to launch campaigns for pure branding. For smaller companies, however, almost every other objective will give better and more significant results.

Reach

When to use it: Similar to the brand awareness goal, the reach objective is functional to reach the maximum number of users to which the ad will show. With the introduction of the rules, Facebook now allows you to put a cap on the frequency with which the ad is shown to the same user; in this sense, the goal for reach becomes very useful when you have to work with a relatively small audience and you want everyone to view the ad.

Traffic

When to use it: When we want to take users to a website, or for example on a landing page. It is a very interesting goal when promoting content, such as a blog post.

Leads

When to use it: The lead ads greatly simplify the signup process from mobile devices. When someone clicks on the ad, a form opens with all personal contact information already pre-filled based on the information they share on Facebook, such as name, surname, phone and email address. This aspect makes the process really fast and within 2 clicks, one to open the ad and one to send the information.

The only problem with this type of objective is that often the email address used to sign up for Facebook several years ago is obsolete and has not been updated for too long. In this case, we would get a useless contact. As a result, it has been seen that better conversion campaigns perform that point to specific external landing pages with data to be filled out.

Another aspect to keep in mind is that lead ads do not allow you to include all the information you want in the offer, like on a landing page. Therefore, for campaigns that require a great deal of cognitive attention from the user, a campaign for conversions will be more successful. That said, in any case, it is always better to do a test between the two approaches and see which performs better, because each case and sector can behave differently.

The success of a Facebook campaign depends almost entirely on how we select the right target. Good results are not obtained by trying to guess the interests but only by experimenting and testing. And knowing the right tools.

- The pixel of Facebook.

Fabio Sutto, a Facebook expert, says it is categorical. The pixel of Facebook should always be installed anyway, even if at the moment we are not interested in campaigning and even if we believe we do not need anything. But why? Because when it is installed (by entering a code on our website), it starts recording data. The pixel will then be able to make us reach users who come into contact with our site, and these users can be used in future for our listings. It must be installed "regardless" because we may regret not having collected the data when these will help us.

- Spy on competitors' sponsorships.

Coming into an advertisement published by our competitors can be a golden opportunity. We can "spy" the target they have chosen for their sponsorship. Just clicking on the 'Why do I view this ad?', the magic is accomplished — we will see exactly what target has set our competitor.

Whether the interests that our competitor has selected works or not, we do not know, however, we can get an idea based on the vanity metrics. And in any case, we now have some tools to test. Below are images taken from Fabio Sutto's slides that illustrate how we can exploit the sponsorships of others.

First, click on "Why do I view this listing?"

- Create a personalized audience.

Facebook gives us many options to intercept our

potential customers, and we should always start with our customers or our traffic. For example, we can upload a file with our LinkedIn contacts or newsletter subscribers, we can take advantage of the pixel and select who visits specific pages of the site or generate events (such as sales or add to cart), who spends more time on the site or who visit him more often, or who opens the newsletter.

- Take advantage of other channels, like AdWords.

The ads on Facebook certainly do not answer any conscious question. We launch the bait to a potentially interested public and hope that someone will realize that they need our product or service. With ads on AdWords, we intercept the conscious need; the user needs the tires and searches on Google, find our ad, and land on our site.

Well, we can take advantage of the results obtained from AdWords. Such as? Just leave the pixel of Facebook "listening" and with the data obtained, create our custom audience based on traffic on the site. At that point, the user who has seen our model X of tires but who has not completed the purchase will see "chased" from our product even within Facebook.

- Use A/B testing.

The analysis of the results obtained must always be exploited to our advantage. Facebook gives us the opportunity with A/B testing.

Facebook Campaigns: Rules to Define the Budget

The risk of wasting money on Facebook campaigns is very high. To avoid spending our money badly, there are a series of precautions that it is best to undertake.

Rules to improve CPAs (cost per action) by working on the budget:

- Do not choose too ambitious self-optimization goals. This is especially true for e-commerce, but it is always applicable. It takes a number of daily conversions high enough for campaigns to be able to learn effectively and improve their performance. We use micro-conversions, i.e. intermediate conversions that are easier to obtain.

- Head different configurations (see advanced planning). When the available budget allows it and "we are allowed to make mistakes", it is good to test different configurations in order to find the ideal setting.

- Increase the budget progressively. When a campaign proves to be performing, it is normal to want to increase the budget allocated to it and make it climb, however, the increase must be progressive and for small steps (10% - 20%). Or, if there is urgency, better clone the campaign and create a new one with the desired budget. Otherwise, 9/10 there is an increase in CPC and a general decline in performance

- Do not accept default placements. Always separate positions in groups with the same target until proven otherwise.

Facebook Leads: How to Get Quality Leads

Do not stop at the lead, look for the quality of the contact. Landing pages generate higher quality contacts because they intercept through questions and require a commitment to fill out the forms, and the quality is paid (with CPL, costs per lead, high).

The Facebook lead ads have unparalleled CPLs, but the quality is affected. The Facebook form is pre-filled with the user's data and often the latter submits without giving weight to the action, perhaps even just out of curiosity. That's why the ads should never use insertions and forms that are too simple. Indeed, complex forms, in which we challenge the user with questions (or even propose a quiz), can have a considerable engagement.

Among the various platforms to start implementing social media marketing activities, Facebook tends to be one that best meets the marketing objectives of a company.

Numbers are important, but not all count in the same way. The data have no value in itself; they only have it if they are functional to trigger processes of understanding and improvement of our actions. When it comes to analyzing the activities undertaken on social networks and making reports to understand how it is going, between Internal Insights and External Tools, the feeling is sometimes to get lost in counting and not being able to get some useful information to act better. Today, we see which values should be kept under control with the Insights that Facebook gives us for free.

So, let's go to the point. What are the most important Facebook Insight metrics? Obviously, it depends. It depends on the objectives and KPIs we have set ourselves. From Facebook Insight, these are the categories available to us:

- OVERVIEW: The overview.

In the overview, we immediately realize the progress of our activities in the last week and three fundamental values for the algorithm of Facebook; Like, Cover, and Engagement. We have a general overview of the volume of Like, the coverage achieved by our posts, and the Engagement generated with our activities on the Page.

From the "Export" button, at the top right, in the same bar where we find the Insights, Facebook provides us with quarterly data, exportable in an Excel file. Of course, it would be nice to select the time frame that we need to analyze and compare it, for example, with the previous one, but we still cannot do it, as we can see in the screenshot below.

- VOLUMES: Like and post coverage.

In the Like and Reach section, we provide quantitative information that allows us to monitor fan growth and coverage of our posts.

To understand what percentage of fans actually reached out to us, in the Post -> All types of posts section, you can view the percentage of posts in percentage, split between Fans/Non-Fans, passing over the mouse pointer.

- FEEDBACK: The much loved (and feared) interaction.

For every published post that is a link, a photo or a video or simply text, our desire is always the same; to engage the fans. Recently, Facebook has updated the algorithm inserting as a metric of evaluation of the interest aroused, the time spent to visualize a content, even if not explicitly interacting. We do not know how this variable will affect the trend of the pages, but if it were inserted in the Insights, it could become another important value to keep under control.

For now, in the section Posts -> All post published, we can see in percentage the rate of involvement by type of post which is very useful to understand what kind of content you like most to our fans. Just flag the Engagement Rate option, as shown in the screenshot below.

The rate of involvement does not express qualitatively what kind of involvement it is, and, on the Web, you know, it does not work "as long as you talk about it". This data should be associated with the sentiment analysis which involves a search for specific user-generated content and detects whether the engagement is positive or negative.

In the Reach/Like section, we have an overview of the negative feedback:

- o   Hide post.
- o   Hide all posts.
- o   Report as Spam.
- o   I do not like it anymore.

This type of information is not to be ignored, as is often done for "unpleasant" feedback. On the contrary, there are very useful to understand how our work is going. But what we are interested in knowing, in particular, is what kind of content has generated negative actions. To understand this, we have to go to the Posts section and flag the hidden posts, hide all the posts, report as spam.

- TIME: Tell me how long.

Now, we come to a question that cyclically comes back to haunt the Social Media Manager; when is it better to publish? To answer this question, Facebook gives us a screen with the times in which our fans are online. Here, online does not mean that they are on our page or when they usually display our posts. They are simply on Facebook. The question of the best time to publish is somewhat controversial.

To understand when it is better to publish our posts, we can only *test, test, and test*. We plan the types of content and test the success, keeping the typology but changing the time of publication, we repeat the tests over and over again and we will have more concrete indications on the real online presence of our audience.

- COMPETITOR: See how good others are.

Once the metrics have been identified; fan growth, fans/non-fans coverage, engagement by type of posts, negative feedback and publication time, we must also keep them under control for our competitors.

Facebook gives us the opportunity to follow 5 competitor pages and watch how they perform. If you're wondering, yes, the competitor page administrator will be notified once the Page is added to the "Page to watch".

The production of content for Facebook goes hand in hand with the constant analysis of our performances. Let's not forget to spend some time studying Analytics, the best creative ideas can often come from there!

Let's face it, the best way to achieve important results in the e-commerce world (and not only) is to combine the theoretical and practical study with an analysis of real cases. Obviously, it is difficult to find such material around. Those few who do it sell it at a high price. I have come to pay thousands of dollars to be able to see with my own eyes how 100k per month campaigns are managed.

Today, I would like to take a look at one of my Ad Accounts and show you the characteristics of a

1000$ campaign a month. What I want to do today is to share the way in which I stop on Facebook and turn a campaign of 20/30 pieces into one of the thousands of units sold per month.

Many of you have already experienced what it means to have a product for your hands that you like, have the first sales but do not know then how to go beyond that limit of saturation that we all know very well. And so, I hope these posts can be useful to turn some of you into a future power seller.

In the post, use of acronyms. If you are new and you have difficulty, here is a little legend of acronyms:

- PPE: Goal Page Post Engagement
- WC: Objective Website Conversion
- WC LC: Website Conversion objective optimized for Link Click
- WC ATC: Target Website Conversion optimized for Add To Cart
- WC P: Website Conversion objective

optimized for Purchase

- CA: Custom Audience
- LAL: LookAlike (Similar Audience)

I often start with an EPP and a hot targeting on fans of my page, friends of the fans intersected with a broad interest (after speaking in person, one of the smart.ly engineers are less and less inclined to intersections but in some cases, I still use them), Custom Audience on ATC events (Add To Cart) or Purchase related to the account, etc.

I use the EPP as an "entry" (in this screenshot, you only see the WC) because I try to always create engagement around a new product even if I already know the niche and often risk not to go in ROI in this first phase.

Remember that the auction mechanism on Facebook is based on 2 main factors; your bid + engagement. For this reason, even today, I prefer to move like this:

PPE -> WC LC -> WC ATC -> WC P

I do not change what wins for a subsequent optimization. If a WC LC works, I do not go to an ATC WC at most in parallel if the audience is big, but I never close what it sells.

If something does not work or I have a high cost per purchase, I'll try the subsequent optimizations (duplicating and closing the previous ones) and if I do not get anything, I close.

I can work with small or large segments even though as you know, by now, I prefer to use large volumes and rely on the algorithm of FB. But since it does not always work, text also the small audiences.

If I'm over 200/300k, I'll go to Manual Bid while for small audiences, I'll go to Auto Bid. Obviously, this is my method and it is not the only one! Be elastic and put your project at the center, more than any advice, read in some group (yes, even here). Use this post (and others) to inspire and think about your project from another point of view.

- FEATURES OF A WINNING CAMPAIGN: RETARGETING

As you can see from the screenshot, retargeting techniques generate more than 50% of sales.

I use various strategies:

o Retargeting to CA (first two lines): The simplest retargeting of all, the one that I explain in the basic course. Actually, it is based on that principle, but it is structured in such a way as to show different contents after a few days. In this campaign, I segmented CAs over two periods. I have recently started segmenting them in 4 periods. Confusion? I promised you a video about this technique, but I saw a few people interested.

o VIDEO Retargeting: This is a technique that I have felt for a long time and I consider it excellent. It works often and is perfect in all those situations where you have poor initial targeting. Take a video of interest. One of those with a lot of engagement. If you can, edit it in a different way and extrapolate the basic concepts and insert them in a single campaign. Post it to the page and create a Video Views campaign with this post. 3-5 $ a day for 48h or even more if it works. Create a LAL from this audience and start bombarding them with a WC LC and then WC ATC and so on. The third adset in the image was generated by a viral video that has had more than 10,000 shares and has been running for months.

o Retargeting on page/post interaction: This type of retargeting is working a lot. This strategy is implemented by constantly posting viral content on the page (use PostPlanner) and using the new tools you find in audiences. I often work "People Engaged with the post" and usually imposed a window of 60 days. If you have different numbers with other settings, I would love to know your tests on this topic.

o ATC retargeting no purchase: It almost always works. This is one of the reasons why I open an account for every niche I try to scale massively. Create a CA of the ATCs to which you remove the Purchase. In this way, you make a retargeting on all those who have left the cart. Offer an incentive (discount).

- THE SECRET WEAPON: THE LOOKALIKE (LAL)

This is really an amazing strategy and I'd love to meet a Facebook engineer to be able to talk with him about it. The artificial intelligence behind these algorithms is, in my opinion, disconcerting. When I was studying AI at the university, I never thought I could see such applications someday.

How do I start? From LAL 1% on CA visits. I do it more or less when I see a CA of 50-100. But it is not a rule.

WARNING: It takes patience. They are sets that

update every 6 hours depending on the audience's responses to your ads. If you use well, they improve day after day, but they need time to improve. So, do not close them right away especially if you see that the engagement improves day after day. As you have seen, I use the LAL in all sauces (VIDEO, Post / Page Engagement retargeting and others).

- MANAGE COSTS AND INCREASE ROI: Manual Bidding

Well, what about the mechanism that has transformed my way of climbing campaigns? It's difficult to explain in this post all the tricks I use but I'm trying to do it in the group by answering when I can your specific cases.

What I want to do here is to respond to those who are afraid to raise the budget in the manual (some of you in these days had expressed this fear). Remember that increasing the budget of an adset to $500/$1000 a day is not the same as spending them all! This happens if you go to Auto Bid but in manual bidding, things change! Apart from some retargeting adset, the others are in the manual bid and each has about $ 500 a day budget. If your fears were founded, this WC campaign would make me spend more $ 5,000 a day with a return of only 30k. Clearly, use this system only if you know what you're doing.

Common Mistakes for Beginners

The main reason is represented by an imposing and transversal critical mass (over 122 million users in America) that is unmatched in any other social network, within which a large part of its potential audience is likely to be present.

If we add to this a very low access threshold (you can monetize already sustained media investments such as photos, articles, videos etc.) and some interesting advertising possibilities, it becomes easy to see how the Californian colossus has become one of the favorite platforms of Worldwide.

Precisely with the advantages listed, however, planning an editorial activity on a corporate Facebook page can become a source of clamorous mistakes, misunderstandings with its customers and gaffes that are difficult to remedy, capable of shaking even the most authoritative brands.

In this chapter, we list some of the major mistakes that any brand about to start a business on Facebook should keep in mind and try to avoid.

1) Not having a strategy.

People's own content page is an activity that, to bring concrete results, must be programmed with accuracy, according to criteria of efficiency (e.g. availability of multimedia material) and effectiveness (e.g. contents that stimulate the involvement of users), creating the mix that best lends itself to stimulate your audience and reach the set goals.

Basing its presence solely on the dissemination of commercial content, for example, the repeated links to product/service pages are one of the temptations in which it is not only easier to fall, but which only results in the early loss of interest in comparison of the brand by their fans.

2) Not having defined goals.

Improvisation is, in particular, in the field of social media marketing, one of the mistakes most often made by companies, often because of the apparent ease of use of many platforms and / or tools.

This rule also applies to Facebook. Approaching the platform without having considered the most appropriate strategy to follow, and without having first defined clear, specific, and measurable objectives to pursue, it means starting an activity that will be completely same, if not counterproductive.

3) Not having a posting schedule.

Finding the right timing to publish your updates is an essential element to determine your visibility on Facebook. Understanding the most correct frequency certainly requires some time (and attempts), since it varies according to the relevant public (there is no rule applicable to all).

In this way, however, we will be able to maximize

the visibility of our posts, avoiding too large editorial "holes" or, on the contrary, of clogging the Home Page of our contacts with too close updates, with the risk of losing the acquired fans and coming "hidden" "from the respective news flows.

Common Mistakes for Intermediates

When you are an intermediate Facebook marketer, there are two main mistakes that you risk making. Correcting them as soon as possible is the first step to get to the next level.

1) Do not remember the balance between performance and results.

I find that mentally splitting the campaign objectives between performance and results is the most effective starting point.

Remember, in Facebook, "performance" is all that at the campaign level aims to increase the yield in terms of Likes, Comments, Shares, and Reproductions of content that lives on the social. On the other hand, "results" goes to cover all those campaigns that aim to bring the user on the site and monitor, possibly, conversions.

This is the enormous strength of Facebook; being able to tap into a social context to direct people to an external site, or vice versa. Thus, some of the questions to be asked become; (1) when do I need to track the performance of a Facebook content; and (2) when do I need to track results, in terms of leads collected on a landing?

In this sense, collecting Likes for a brand page becomes just a piece of the puzzle. A campaign with this goal is just the first step to deliver a targeted editorial strategy to this fan base. Or maybe use this audience in a second campaign, this time with the goal "Address people to your website". Or develop a similar audience again.

In the same way, increasing the visualizations of a video allows you to think first of the performance (the reproductions obtained, of course) and on a horizon to results, building a list of audiences based precisely on the percentages of reproduction.

Before thinking about ad creativity, mentally divide the opportunities given by Facebook in terms of performance and results is the best (and really strategic) way to proceed.

2) Ignore the new features.

One of the best adjectives to describe Facebook Ads is "seething". In eternal modification and improvement, new features are screaming loudly, especially among industry professionals. In other cases, they pass undertone or are released in installments without precise timing.

Taking advantage of the opportunities offered by any new ad setup or bidding mechanics is especially important when it comes to refinements that are still young, of which we do not know any future but that could bring interesting results. Arriving first, in this case, is an opportunity not to be missed.

Common Mistakes for Advanced Facebook Marketers

1) Not being reactive.

Do not assume that what works today can continue to do so without changes in the coming times. Be ready to push (even at the budget level) what works, seizing the opportunities when they arise.

Come back to your campaigns as often as possible, look at reports critically, and above all, be ready to change your mind. It's not always that the most creative ad is the one that converts the best. Not always the call-to-action that you have retouched for a long time is the most effective. The ego has nothing to do with it; you only look at the results.

2) Not dividing the campaign by placements.

Facebook does its best to give as much exposure as possible to its advertisers' ads. However, this visibility does not always coincide with the best context to make our message effective.

Dividing each campaign at least between desktop and mobile is the basis for avoiding a dispersion of the message across multiple fronts. Refine the message between smartphone and tablet the next step.

With the progressive development of Facebook Ads, it is not uncommon to find campaigns automatically addressed to the news feed on desktop, mobile, tablet, within Instagram and on the audience network. Separate, as much as possible, each front with different creativities and approaches, even at the budget level.

Some advice?

The desktop news feed is great for generating engagement since it supports longer texts and more readable descriptions. The mobile news feed is more effective to reach a target that does not yet know us, bringing the first click on a landing and allowing us to act in remarketing in the medium term. The right-hand column is always less efficient, but often cheaper and still useful in remarketing contexts. The audience network is interesting as an opportunity to collect clicks from in-target users, but it is scarcely relevant to point directly to conversions. The positioning on Instagram is everything to test niche for niche, but realistically it can work better on more emotional contexts.

3) Not testing different creatives and levers.
Not all messages work the same way. Especially when there is not a real campaign historian or other marketing strategies that can provide a canvas are not active; the real challenge is to grasp which "form" has the ideal announcement for those who receive it.

Experimenting, in this case, is a must. Head different images, with different tones, with or without people inside. Evaluate more or less long texts and the presence or absence of links. Changes the call to the action present under the content (if the campaign goal allows it). Different colors with different intensities could bring out or bury your ad regardless of the message.

Do not just offer a single ad and see clicks; conversions and cost reports arrive. It is not satisfactory. The goal is to understand what is the best cost/result ratio that can be achieved and with which creativity.

Chapter 6: The Importance of Instagram in 2019

How to Succeed on Instagram

Instagram is a rather unusual social networking platform which is unlike with the other social networks such as Facebook or Twitter, thanks also to the lower average age of users, a more informal behavior, characterized by immediacy and sharing of the moment.

Instagram is therefore increasingly used in synergy with other social networks to highlight a less serious part of the brand linked to the story, to people, to life, and in short, to "behind the scenes"; or to show a more "creative" side linked to the playful and artistic aspect.

Using a Business Account

Business profiles arrived in Italy in June 2016 and brought very useful news for all companies that use Instagram in their social media marketing strategy.

If you are a freelancer or a company, if you have not already done so, the thing we recommend is to immediately switch the switch. Simply enter the settings and tap on "Switch to Business Profile". At this point, you will not have to do anything but associate the linked Facebook page and indicate the contact options such as email and phone number.

By providing this data correctly, when users will land on your Business profile, they will be able to contact you directly without too many steps; just tap on "Call" or "Email". In addition, for the companies that have activated the Instagram shopping function, the item "Products" will appear.

Once the switch is made to Business Profile, at the top right, a graphic icon will appear, namely the Insights.

The data shown are as follows:

- Impression and reach of your posts.
- Photos with more interactions.
- Insights data on Instagram Stories.
- Data on followers.
- Insights related to promotions.

Instagram Biography: How to Write It

To implement a marketing strategy on Instagram, it is necessary to start from the details, that is the care of the biofield.

It is important to know that within this section it is mandatory to be as clear as possible, using the keywords that best identify the sector to which the company belongs. Recently, the platform introduced the possibility of inserting hashtags into the bio, making profiles easier to find.

The Instagram biography can contain a maximum of 150 characters and must be written with extreme care because, together with the profile image, this is what will prompt the user to click on the "Follow" button and on the Call to Action.

Tone of Voice

First, it is necessary to define a Tone of Voice consistent with the values of the brand, but which is in line with the target audience, that is the potential members of the community. To define the ToV, it is necessary to build a social media monitoring activity, that is the monitoring of user conversations.

This type of activity can be verified through suitable online tools such as Radian, Socialbakers, and many others.

Listening to conversations that revolve around certain keywords is useful for your Instagram Marketing strategy. It will be of fundamental importance to understand how users express themselves and what problems and needs they would like to see resolved. All this is essential when studying a digital communication strategy.

Emojis

The use of emoji is by no means a child's practice, on the contrary, they can be used as a creative list for the division of application fields.

The visual content attracts much more than the text, consequently putting emoticons that help to outline the bio, is a way to get the user's attention.

Another trick is to wrap between sentences, to better clarify who you are, what you do and call to action to the user.

CTA - Call to Action

In an Instagram Marketing strategy, it is always necessary to include a clear call to action to users. "Visit our website" or "Follow us on Facebook and Twitter" are CTA in all respects and it is necessary that the message is clear to users and traceable to the company through, for example, a tracking code of Google Analytics.

The Importance of Storytelling

Why has visual storytelling become fundamental in any digital strategy? Recent research has shown that users have an average attention threshold of 8 seconds. This shows the need for companies to be able to create attractive tools to ensure that the user's eye stops to read and watch content.

Storytelling means telling stories for persuasive communication, especially in politics, economics, and business. With the advent of social networks, users want to read and see original stories. This is why companies are required continuous innovation in the art of storytelling and emotion.

Self-referencing does not pay any more. It is necessary to use tools like Instagram to create narrative universes useful for community involvement.

To be able to create a good strategy for Instagram Marketing, it is of fundamental importance to experiment to find the correct and most appreciated way by the users. The feed created must be homogeneous so as not to confuse the community, which means that if you deal with catering, it makes no sense to publish travel content or other topics not closely related.

To have a good following on Instagram, you have to

start from a good visual content. If the content is interesting and engaging, users will stop to read the caption or the caption. Within this field, it is necessary to tell stories involving the microblogging technique.

Instagram (like Facebook) offers fairly frequent news such as video 60 seconds, Instagram Stories, photo albums, and IGTV. Therefore, it is always experimenting with new techniques for creating engagement within the community.

Speaking of video 60 seconds, if you have included them in your strategy, we recommend using Instagram video apps like Boomerang, Diptic or Flipagram.

Create a Content Marketing Strategy on Instagram

The first thing to do, once we have identified our target audience, is to structure the right content marketing strategy.

In fact, it is not enough to "be on Instagram" to be able to say to use this medium. Rather, it is necessary to study a path, also creative, that allows the user who follows the brand to receive interesting contents, obviously respecting the Tone of Voice and the image and positioning of the company and that, through this path, we can bring user to become an ambassador and customer of the company.

To give a concrete (and simple) example, if the company is in the food sector, you will have to create a content marketing strategy that aims to give culinary directions such as recipes, ingredients, raw materials. The contents should not be strictly related to the sale of the product but must serve to create an interaction and a relationship of trust with the user, who will then be interested in accessing the social network also because it finds interesting content on the company feed.

Create an Editorial Plan and an Editorial Calendar

Once a clear content marketing strategy has been identified, shared with all team members, we can proceed to summarize what has been decided so far within the editorial plan for the social network. It means creating a document with objectives, targets, and ways of creating content within a document that becomes the guide to consistently create future content to be posted on Instagram.

These contents will be programmed and inserted into an editorial calendar. Having an editorial calendar is essential because it allows you to never run out of content, as these are decided on a time, with certain deadlines and with equally certain managers.

An editorial calendar is therefore made up of specific posts, inserted into a weekly and monthly calendar, to be followed to make sure you never run out of post. Ideally, if we believe we have enough content, we could also post on Instagram every day, which means structuring an editorial calendar that needs to have several months already covered. It is, however, desirable to have a calendar that requires posting two or three times a week.

Interact with Followers and Create a Community

Creating a community on Instagram is very important to create a Comment Marketing activity, a strategy based on comments on photos similar to those published by your company. The use of Instagram Bot is increasingly frequent, allowing follow-up and commenting based on who uses specific hashtags within the caption.

The problem of Comment Marketing with the Bots is that it does not lead to the real creation of the community, as a simple "Nice" or a little heart is not enough to really interact with the relevant public. For this reason, for the creation of a community, it is always better to search through hashtag photos in line with your brand and to comment on them manually and regularly, writing something that also leads to an answer and intrigues the user so much to push them to follow you in turn.

How to Use Influencers

What are the influencers? Influencers are people with a significant following on Instagram, who may then have the power to direct users who follow them to a particular brand or company.

In fact, influencers are usually rather sectorial and followed assiduously by those who are interested in a specific topic, so they can contact to look for a relationship with their own brand if the target between their followers and those of the company is coherent. You can structure a co-marketing strategy with a shared hashtag or, in the case of companies in the fashion industry, for example, use them as brand ambassadors through their posts. In case of events (such as festivals or other events), they can be invited to create awareness on the specific event.

Create Contest on Instagram

The creation of a contest on Instagram is a very widespread practice to stimulate the engagement in the community already formed, for the improvement of the brand awareness and for the generation of new qualified leads.

Stimulating Competition

For participation in an Instagram contest, users must feel encouraged to share personal photographs with a decidedly large network. In order to convince and involve the community, it is necessary to have a stimulating idea that will somehow leverage the emotional sphere of the individual.

An example of an emotional contest can be that of Vetoquinol, where users have been asked to take up moments of play and fun with their four-legged friend.

Interesting Prizes

When users decide to participate in an online competition, it is very easy for them to try to win the prize at stake. The greater the perceived value (economic and / or effectivity), the greater the chances of participation by users.

If the company deals with sales of technological products, the raffling of the latest tablet model released on the market will be more incentive than the awarding of simple custom covers.

Furthermore, the prizes of a competition must always be in line with the promoter's core business, to avoid confusing users about your field of activity.

Studying a Promotion Strategy

In addition to the classic promotional strategies such as ADV, newsletters, postings on the page, and shares, on Instagram, you can use the hashtags. Each competition must have its own hashtag designed for the occasion, which allows to group in a simple way all the contents published by the users.

Instagram Stories: How to Exploit Them

The Instagram Stories were introduced in the second half of 2016, after witnessing the Snapchat boom especially in the very young audience (target between 15 and 25 years).

The Stories have potentials thanks to their usability. They serve to offer special contents that disappear after 24 hours. When applied to Instagram Marketing, this can be very useful, as you can create exclusive content for creating engagement within particular communities.

For example, you can use them to show moments of exclusive events to engage the fanbase or to offer special discounts and promotions lasting only 24 hours. Or again, if you have a verified Instagram profile, you will have the opportunity to show the products offered by the online shop by entering the direct link. This way, you will not require too many steps to users, who will feel more incentive to proceed with the purchase.

This technique is often used by blogger and entrepreneur Chiara Ferragni, who in her stories, mixes moments of everyday life with decidedly more commercial content in which she shows the products she designed and created, referring directly to her e-shop.

Features like questions, surveys, and emoji appreciation have made them even more interactive, contributing to the enormous success that Instagram Stories are having between users and companies.

How to Measure the Results

The strategy of creating an Instagram profile is useful. Set goals, periodically go to check if those objectives, medium, and long-term, have been respected. You will then check, in addition to the mere and simple "engagement" on the platform, if those followers have also become customers or users of our product.

In order to measure the results, it is important to have correctly set the conversion funnel and be able to obtain quantifiable data from the analytics platforms set. If the goal is to make sure that users register for a service on our site, it will be important to identify how many users have come through our Instagram channel.

Chapter 7: YouTube Marketing in 2019

The promotion through YouTube will be one of the biggest opportunities that this social platform makes available in 2019 and through the right skills, we will know how to enhance and take the best of what YouTube offers us.

Success comes through YouTube views, visits obtained by watching that specific video or that specific channel. In this case, every user registered on the platform, (after the marriage with Google, just a Big G account), can become (in one fell swoop) a publisher, author, director and screenwriter of their YouTube channel, which will be instantly reachable throughout the world and official disseminator of your ideas. Or you can decide to become simply a spectator with decidedly active connotations, together with many other viewers; means the success of a video or of the same YouTube channel, and also a reflection of a brand or an idea. The YouTube views are therefore the number of views that the video gets, not to be confused with the YouTube Likes, which instead indicate your liking related to the video or channel viewed.

The second concept is not entirely different from what made Facebook famous and is one of the first parameters to keep in mind to achieve success. Making a video and uploading it to YouTube is easy, but it is even easier to end up in obscurity and never reach the desired visibility. Our goal is to provide the right information not to end up in a dead end and not remain anonymous.

Whether you are a company or a private individual with a new idea, we have the means of promotion for your YouTube Marketing and we are able to offer you a solid marketing plan. As with any product, even YouTube has its own good rules and its good techniques to stay on the crest of the wave and we study and apply it daily.

YouTube SEO have some basic steps to follow, not to

be one of many on the video sharing platform, but to be among the protagonists, offering greater visibility on search engines. Among the measures made available, we mention some that may seem trivial, but they are all important to get to the top and stay there.

The metadata is undoubtedly fundamental, that is all the additional information we can give as a part of our video. The descriptions to the video and to the YouTube Channel are an example but subtitles, if present, and is used as an indexing parameter for a video (the same speech is intended to be extended in the same way between channel and video).

An accurate description in the process of creating the channel, and uploading the video in short, should not be taken lightly, but rather must be carefully studied and weighted. It is the place where billions of people place their eyes every day. The interesting fact is that these eyes do not belong only to a particular category of people, but to every population.

You will certainly understand what this could mean for your company's marketing. But how do you effectively

JACK GARY

use this channel to promote and grow your business? Let's browse a bit between the channels of this Social Network and see what we can understand.

YouTube is full of quirky videos, often frivolous and sometimes meaningless (at least in appearance), loaded mainly by teenagers or young adults.

Chapter 8: How to Grow Organically on YouTube

TIP 1: PUBLISH CONTENT, NOT ADVERTISEMENT

You'll soon realize that traditional forms of advertising do not work on YouTube. You'll have to experiment with other ways to advertise your e-commerce, your site or your company.

Not even company presentation videos or product demos give great results unless they are particularly creative.

When you create video content to upload to this channel, take time to reflect on why and how your audience should appreciate it and share it. The shareability factor is indeed as important as the underlying idea and the quality of its realization.

TIP 2: BECOME THE FACE OF YOUR BUSINESS

YouTube is a community of real people who want to give in, feel, and interact with other real people. The link with your company or with your brand is greatly strengthened if the public can associate a face, preferably the most representative of the entire organization.

This move can profoundly change the dynamics of interaction, going from watching a company video to building a relationship with a human being. Aiming at the establishment of interpersonal relationships, therefore, becomes a long-term strategy that can make your company gain life for customers.

The face of the company must obviously appear as much as possible, in the videos but also in the header of your channel and in the previews of the contents. Another winning strategic move is to include splits of personal life within your business if there is not too much force. Allow your audience to peek behind the scenes, to see your project take shape or to discover how you started this profession. This transparency adds depth and color to your marketing.

TIP 3: ALL COME FROM ZERO

Many users who begin to use YouTube for their company's marketing open a channel, upload a couple of content and soon get discouraged because they do not achieve the desired goals in terms of subscriptions and views. From the initial enthusiasm, they, therefore, pass to abandon the enterprise, with a fair load of frustration.

Gathering an audience around your YouTube channel is a process that takes time and patience. Focus on creating valuable content and in the best possible quality. Promote your channel, announce it on your blog, on your mailing lists, and on the other social platforms on which you are present. Also, include a YouTube sharing button in the above-the-fold area of your website.

As you do everything in your power to promote your channel and videos, remember to interact with the followers you've already won. Take care of these people who, in a boundless sea of possibilities, have chosen to follow you. Reply to any postman comments if possible, on the community ASAP and, if they have a channel, visit it and comment it in turn.

TIP 4: BRING USERS TO YOUR SITE

For most businesses, a YouTube Marketing strategy cannot stop attracting subscribers and views. Of course, this is the first of the goals, but once achieved, there must be a further step towards converting these users into customers. To do this, you will probably need to create a bridge between YouTube and your site.

Include a link to your site in the first line of each description you write for your videos. Enter a link to the About Us section of your site in the header of your channel.

Study methods for making the user move to your site, such as a two-part video of which the first is available on YouTube and the second only on one of your company web pages.

TIP 5: FIND COLLABORATIONS

Another very effective tactic to empower your efforts on YouTube is to collaborate with an established designer. This can happen in different ways and forms, but for most companies, it will probably involve investing a certain budget to offer to one of the most and well-targeted YouTube for your goals.

Take some time to select candidates. Choose between those who have at least 100,000 subscribers and who exercise a significant ascendancy on your target audience. Once you have identified your influencer, you can make different proposals; create a video according to your requests, appear in one of your videos, talk about yourself or your products in one of his productions.

These characters are generally very protective of their community and the role they have won. They are therefore understandably very selective in evaluating the opportunities for collaboration that they receive. Offer them something that they can genuinely feel in their chords and you will be more likely to receive positive feedback.

147

TIP 6: SEO IS IMPORTANT

YouTube is the second largest search engine after Google which is also a brother since 2006, and the two get along very well. Although the Google algorithm is almost top secret, it seems that a YouTube video, with the appropriate metadata compiled properly, has more ease to acquire a high ranking compared to a blog post equally optimized.

Not only can your videos appear among Google search results, but they also do so with a thumbnail that provides a visual preview of the content.

TIP 7: DO NOT FORGET THE CALL TO ACTION

This is an essential point when it comes to using YouTube for professional reasons. If it is possible during, but no doubt at the end of each video, you need to insert a call-to-action. You want your users to take a certain action once your creation is appreciated, right?

The content is, in fact, a tool to capture the attention,

perhaps entertain, inform and create a relationship. At a certain point, however, this attention should flow into something that will also benefit your business. This could be simply filling out a form, sharing the video with your contacts or visiting a specific page of your e-commerce.

The possibilities are endless, and the effectiveness of your choice will also depend on the creativity that you will be able to use in catching them. Consult YouTube policies, make sure your idea is not in opposition to any of the points and then give free space to your inventiveness.

Growing Your YouTube Business

YouTube registers more than a billion unique visitors each month. In the same amount of time, over 6 billion hours of content are used by users. It is clear that, for brands as well as creators, YouTube is an opportunity not to be missed to present, tell, and connect with the public.

Building your presence on the Mountain View video platform cannot disregard the design of a channel that, by structure and content, is able to attract users and encourage them to subscribe.

Notwithstanding that the quality of the contents remains an unavoidable prerogative to achieve this goal, below you will find a list of 13 useful things to do to promote your channel and increase subscribers on YouTube.

1) Promotion on other social channels.

Every social network has its own nature, characteristics, languages, communicative modalities of its own, often different public. Choosing to publish the same content on multiple platforms does not always pay in terms of effectiveness; however, using your own "social spaces" to promote the YouTube channel can be very useful to give the latter wide resonance.

For example, on the Facebook page, you can add a dedicated tab that will allow you to build a video clip generated directly from the channel (you can use services like Woobox). On Pinterest, you could create a special board, or maybe one for each product/topic/collaboration you have posted on YouTube.

2) Email Marketing

Sending periodic emails to your subscribers can be very useful to notify you when a new video is released, or to bring your attention back to less recent but significant footage.

YouTube does not allow you to send an email notification directly to your subscribers (They are, in fact, the latter to manage from their profile; the ability to receive notifications when favorite channels upload new videos.); however, using your site or blog, you can build a database by landing the viewers here and asking them for their email address in exchange for valuable content (such as an eBook, a report, etc.).

3) Video Ads

YouTube video ads are a good opportunity to make yourself known as they allow you to select your target audience based on gender, age, interests, and location. You can choose from among different ad formats the one that best suits your needs.

4) SEO Optimization

There are many practices recommended by YouTube to improve the placement of videos and channels, from the inclusion of keywords in the title and description to the use of subtitles, until the creation of playlists.

5) Connect the channel to site and / or blog.

If your activity involves the use of a website or a blog, it may be useful to insert links to the YouTube channel (provided that it is here that you want to get users and this operation does not risk cannibalizing visits to your site main).

Creating a custom button is very simple thanks to the easy to understand configurator that YouTube makes available.

Embed the videos inside the pages or insert the subscription button.

6) Collaborations

The collaborative videos are born from the work of two or more YouTubers. We find examples in which the creatives find themselves in the same recording space and others were, instead, what we see is the result of the editing of two clips generated in different times and spaces.

Whatever the way they are created, this kind of footage increases exponentially the potential visibility of a channel (as long as the public are similar and have similar interests) and proves useful not only for the personal branding of a Creator. Even brands can profitably collaborate with "YouTube stars", reinventing the concept of endorsement to create quality content and is relevant to their audience.

7) Fan Search

This is a free channel promotion service offered by YouTube. Each channel will be able to promote itself by creating a pre-roll announcement. The users to whom it will be shown will be the ones that will most closely approach a detailed profile built on the basis of precise interests.

Each video of the channel can be chosen for this type of announcement, even if the trailer is probably the most suitable for this purpose.

8) Google Hangouts

Hangouts is a Google tool that allows users to make video calls and video conferences (up to 15 people connected).

Google Hangouts also offers many benefits to brands and creators. All video conferencing is broadcast live on your YouTube channel and on Google+, thus expanding the number of people who can (do not actively participate) see the content. Once the live broadcast is finished, the video recording will automatically be uploaded to the channel, available to anyone who wants to use it.

This is a tool certainly useful for presenting new products and content, collaborations, or perhaps to respond to requests from fans.

9) Connected channels.

YouTube offers channel managers the opportunity to highlight other channels that may be particularly interesting for their audience. Using this tool is a good idea to cross-promote other channels with similar or complementary content to yours, or with which collaborate.

In addition to offering content relevant to your audience, interacting genuinely with other creators will increase the chances of being included in their "Featured Channels" lists.

10) Analytics

The statistical tools of YouTube are a great help to measure the performance of video and build or reformulate from them an effective video programming strategy. In addition to the number of views, "Like", "I do not like" comments and shares, you can access other data on your channel regarding display time, traffic sources, subscriber and demographics.

11) Originality of the contents.

Despite the commitment and perseverance in publishing videos, still, you cannot increase your views and subscribers to YouTube? If you treat a particular topic and do it exactly like others do, why should a person look at yours?

If you really do not have new ideas, you can try to look at some foreign format and get ideas, then try to create something totally yours.

12) Give a visual impact to your brand.

Think of your channel as if it was a brand. It must be something recognizable in any context such as YouTube or other social networks, and also on a flyer or gadget. Therefore, be wide to the imagination, choose fonts and colors that they stay well with each other, look for a style, and always remain coherent.

You have to choose a cover and use it on all the channels that you have available, only so that users will be able, over time, to associate your brand with content.

13) Choice of the topic.

There are many generalist YouTube channels which make videos of various kinds, treating a bit of everything, from the news to sports, cinema, and so on. Many think it could be a useful choice to attract audiences of various sectors, however, there is a risk of being very dispersive. On YouTube, there are many channels of this kind, so the best solution is to choose only one topic and treat it. Over time, you will become a point of reference in that specific sector with as much success as possible.

The 3 Mistakes to Avoid at All Costs When It Comes to YouTube

When you subscribe to YouTube, you do it with the hope of breaking through and becoming famous, but you have to take into account several factors such as that of huge competition, so being able to get noticed is not as simple as you think.

There are many YouTubers who want to increase YouTube views and subscribers to their channel, but often make mistakes, even trivial, which lead to the opposite result.

1) Not having a publishing program.

It is important to have a plan to publish content. There are channels that publish many videos every day, and others that are reduced to a couple a year. We are at two extremes that do not bring any kind of benefit.

In fact, uploading too many videos is not good, because the subscribers find the home clogged by the contents and many may decide to remove the subscription to the channel, moreover, making such a large number of videos could decrease the quality of content and topics covered.

On the other hand, doing only a couple of videos a year does not help to build the audience and build a network of subscribers because people will forget about the existence of the channel.

The right solution? It's in the middle, like all things. There are no precise numbers, much depends on the format. The important thing is to never give up quality. The more beautiful the videos are, the more they are appreciated. A couple a week could be the right choice.

2) Not choosing a convincing and impactful name.

Many do not give this the right importance but choosing the name for your YouTube channel is essential because that word will be associated with the project, the face of the creator, and the videos that will be uploaded.

So, before opening a channel, it is good to think carefully about the nickname to be proposed to the potential public. Try to find the word that best summarizes the main topic of your project.

It should be a name that users will remember easily and will immediately associate with the channel when they see a new video uploaded.

3) Having low-quality videos.

The quality of the videos is essential if you want the public to appreciate the published content. In fact, one of the main successes is the user experience. You can also make an interesting video but if you do not understand and do not see well, it will not help.

So, you have to equip yourself with quality equipment, even a normal HD camera, which has a better resolution, is fine.

Chapter 9: YouTube and Money

How to Monetize YouTube and How to Use It in a Social Media Marketing Strategy

Have you ever wondered how to make money with YouTube through videos posted online? I bet yes and if you're here now and you're reading this chapter, it's obviously because you have not yet managed to find a satisfactory answer to your question. If things are actually this way, you know that this time you can count on me too. I can, in fact, provide all the explanations of the case and indicate how to collect the money from your online videos.

To answer immediately your question, know that to earn with YouTube, the only valid system is advertising the ones that are shown before the videos or directly on them. But how do you get them?

Simple, you have to become a YouTube partner.

Having clarified this point, if you are really interested in learning more and discovering all that you can do to make money with YouTube, I suggest you take a few minutes of free time and concentrate on reading this tutorial. I do not promise that at the end of this chapter you will become a "maharajah" thanks to your videos posted on the net but certainly, you will have much clearer ideas on how to earn some money thanks to the videos posted on the net on the famous Google platform. So, are you ready? Yes? Very well, so we ban the chatter and start.

As I said, to be able to earn on YouTube, it is essential to becoming a partner of the site. To be accepted in the program, you need to have a fair number of views, many videos uploaded to the channel and do not have to infringe on copyright or the internal rules of YouTube. If you think you have all the credentials, try it. It costs nothing.

Before giving you all the explanations on the case of how to become a partner of the popular video portal and, therefore, on how to make money with YouTube, however, I want you to keep in mind a fundamental thing. To generate considerable gains, it is also necessary to have a considerable audience. Simply put, there are few, very few, those who manage to "live" only on YouTube (intended as advertising revenue). Many more people are able to make money thanks to the personal promotion that YouTube, with its vast range of public, allows to accomplish. But this is another matter.

Choose a Third-Party Network

Another important factor to take into consideration is that of partnerships with third-party companies. The standard YouTube affiliation, the one I'm going to talk to you about, is only for those who do not have the "tube" star ambition and cannot get very high income.

The so-called YouTube-stars, those that grind tens of thousands of views on each video and count hundreds of thousands of subscribers, rely on external networks that act as intermediaries with the Google portal, which, in exchange for a small percentage on advertising revenue, allow them to receive technical support, promotions to increase views, and extra content (such as copyrighted soundtracks) for use in videos.

To find the most suitable network for your channel, you can search for the services used by the most famous YouTubers using the SocialBlade platform that you can access by clicking *here*. Once you have viewed the main Web page of SocialBlade, just type the username of a YouTuber in the bar at the top right and click on the Search button. That's all.

Regardless of the type of affiliation chosen, YouTube pays videos based on a criterion called CPM (cost per thousand impressions). The sum in money that is paid to those who exploit the advertising on YouTube is therefore linked to how much the sponsors pay and the amount can vary every month. In general, you can still say that for every 1,000 views on a video with advertising, you can get only a few Euros approximately from 5.00 dollars to 7.00 dollars.

How to Become a YouTube Partner

Now, let's move on to the point. If you want to try to make money with YouTube, the first thing you need to do is to connect to the management panel of your account.

Make sure now that the channel for which you hold enjoy a good reputation, both in terms of copyright both in our community standards. Then check that next to the Community Guidelines and Copyright entries, there is a green dot. If it were not so, I'm sorry to tell you but, you will not be able to request the monetization of videos and then earn with YouTube.

In addition to the requirements above, also verify that your channel has reached at least 1,000 subscribers and 4,000 hours in the last 12 months. Otherwise, you will not be able to participate in the YouTube Partner Program (YPP).

Then click on the Activate button next to the Monetization item to send your request to become a partner through monetization by posting ads on your videos.

In the page, at this point, you will be shown the Enable my account button and then add the check to the three boxes at the end of the box displayed in the middle of the web page and then click on the button Accept >>.

Now, choose the available ad formats and then press the Monetize button. Personally, I suggest you leave the checkboxes on the items in-video ads overlay and skippable video ads or in any case, to press on the item Preview to see for good of what it is before performing the deactivation.

If all goes well and you are accepted in the partner program, YouTube will automatically add ads to all your videos. If it is not possible for one or more videos, you will be shown a special notification.

Then, you can still activate banner ads in your videos by accessing your channel's select the video management item located at the top left, putting the check mark next to the movies on which you want to enable monetization, selecting the item Monetize from the Actions menu, and indicating the types of advertising to display in the movies you have chosen.

Know also that before activating the advertising, YouTube will check the content of the videos through a procedure that could last 24-48 hours and, in special cases, may request the sending of information as proof of the fact that you have all the rights to use certain content on a commercial level.

Receive Payments

Payments from standard YouTube affiliation occur only through Adsense (unlike those of third-party networks that can also be through other systems), so before activating ads on your movies, make sure to link your YouTube account with Adsense.

Other Useful Tips

Now that you've finally figured out what you need to do to be able to make money with YouTube, before leaving you free to try to monetize as much as possible with your videos, there are some simple but useful advice that I think is appropriate to give you and that you would do well to take serious consideration.

To make money with YouTube, it is essential to work hard, giving space to talent and creativity. Try to produce something that has real value for the viewer. For this reason, to better understand how to proceed, I suggest you follow what are the most famous YouTube channels and keep an eye on how often by posting new videos and how they interact with fans.

I also suggest that you choose a category of membership for your videos on which you have a good knowledge or for which you have more interest and then try to produce videos that you think can have a real value not only for you but also and especially for others that are able to attract the attention of others because of good quality.

Chapter 10: How to Exploit the Potential of Twitter in 2019

Many people ask how to do marketing on Twitter in 2019 and how to exploit this simple (but powerful) social to promote online communication. Because, after all, this is Twitter, right? A tool to communicate. A tool to track your ideas and your online activity.

With Twitter, you can share text and links, and you can (try to) increase your blog visits. You can post visual content, you can create threads, you can even answer the questions of your followers. Even if you only have 140 characters available, the combinations are endless.

Many believe that to get good results on Twitter, you just have to tweet to promote their content. In reality, it is not so. Behind a good success on Twitter, there is a careful planning of the activities. Those who know this world know it well, but there are rules that everyone should respect to use this social network in the best possible way.

In 2019, Twitter is going to be an important part of every social media marketing strategy, as there are more and more users on the platform every day. In the next two chapters, you are going to discover some amazing strategy to take your Twitter marketing to the next level.

Chapter 11: How to Promote Yourself on Twitter

The basis of Twitter marketing is simple. This social network is made up of conversations, not soliloquies. So, put aside your isolationism. To be able to grasp the results from this social network, you have to interact with people. Or better said, you have to create conversations. You must make sure that there is a natural interest around your brand.

Being human, this is the first rule for those who ask me how to do marketing on Twitter. You cannot hope to get many followers (and many shares) if you continue to live under a glass bell and just post promotional content.

On this social network, visual content is important. You can insert images and videos (both from the desktop and the Twitter application itself), and you can enrich tweets with GIFs. You can activate the big or small Twitter Cards that create a preview of the link you've shared.

The second step is even clearer. You have to become useful. You must become a decisive account for your niche. And you have to do it following the rules of the Twitter algorithm. What is the secret to achieving this goal? I do not believe in secrets, but in good habits. What I recommend is simple; share what people love. Not the contents that are comfortable for you, or at least not only those.

The last step of the path to answering how to do marketing on Twitter is that you have to measure your progress. You must have a clear assessment of your successes or failures. You have to understand what has been lucky and what has been caused by careful planning and create new strategies. You must identify new paths. To do this, you need the statistics.

Once, it was all very difficult but today, Twitter offers complete analytics that platform or meets all needs. To access these pages, go to analytics.twitter.com and start browsing through the various sections.

Remember that conversations are important and the numbers make the difference; not your feelings on how a certain campaign is going.

Chapter 12: How to Do Paid Advertising on Twitter

On Twitter, there are 3 types of promotion. Let's look at them one by one.

Sponsored Tweets

Sponsored Tweets are regular tweets that are promoted by advertisers who want to reach more users to maximize their followers' interaction. When an advertiser pays for a sponsored Twitter, the tweet is shown as "sponsored". For the rest, the Sponsored Tweets are the same as the other tweets and can be retweeted. They can receive Likes and answers.

They can be useful for various reasons for those who want to promote a specific action on Twitter and to increase the popularity of their company. In fact, the sponsored tweet is able to:

- Increase traffic to the website.
- Share coupons and discounts in the tweet text.
- Favor the lead generation through the lead generation page.
- Promote offers and competitions.
- Expand coverage of content, such as blog posts.
- Get in touch with influential people and make sure they see the content.
- Promote awareness in relation to events and product launches.
- Ask to retweet and get an even wider audience.

If a user is not interested in a sponsored Tweet, he can delete it by clicking on the remove button that appears as part of the tweet.

Sponsored Accounts

Sponsored Accounts are intended to suggest an account that people do not yet follow but may find interesting. Their function is clearly to rapidly increase the number of followers, so they are functional when you want to be more identifiable by people who might be interested in their business.

Thanks to Sponsored Accounts, people are able to:

- Increase their sales.
- Increase the number of their leads.
- Increase the popularity of the brand.
- Increase web traffic.

Sponsored Accounts are displayed in different areas of Twitter, such as in the main dashboard, in the "Who to Follow" page and in the search results. Obviously, they will appear only if a Sponsored Account is considered relevant to the user's interests. Sponsored Accounts will also be shown under the "sponsored" label to distinguish them from naturally recommended accounts.

Sponsored Trend

Initially, the Sponsored Trends were born as an extension of the Sponsored Tweet but today, they represent a real autonomous product. Through the Sponsored Trends, users can view advertiser promotions at the top of Twitter's Trend Topics. Even the Promoted Trends are indicated with the "sponsored" label and sometimes they can also appear in users' histories.

The only difference between a natural trend and a Sponsored Trend is the label that indicates the sponsorship of the topic. For the rest, you can click on the trend to view all the tweets that contain the #hashtag and you can tweet including the sponsored trend name in a tweet.

Conclusion

Thank you for making it to the end of this book, we hope it was able to provide you with all the tools you need to achieve your financial goals.

The next step is to get started with what you have learned during the course of this book. Remember; always start by building an audience and creating a positive vibe on your pages. It will make all the difference down the line.

We hope that you find these lessons valuable and that you got the information you were looking for. Creating a "social media lifestyle" that works for you will give you an incredible feeling, especially at the beginning when you make the first gains. We are thrilled for you to start and we cannot wait to see your results coming in.

To your success!

Personal Branding in 2019

Strategies to Build Your Brand With Instagram, Facebook, Youtube and Twitter, Social Media Marketing and Network Marketing

Jack Gary

The following Book is reproduced below with the goal of providing information that is as accurate and reliable as possible. Regardless, purchasing this Book can be seen as consent to the fact that both the publisher and the author of this book are in no way experts on the topics discussed within and that any recommendations or suggestions that are made herein are for entertainment purposes only. Professionals should be consulted as needed prior to undertaking any of the action endorsed herein.

This declaration is deemed fair and valid by both the American Bar Association and the Committee of Publishers Association and is legally binding throughout the United States.

Furthermore, the transmission, duplication or reproduction of any of the following work including specific information will be considered an illegal act irrespective of if it is done

way be considered an endorsement from the trademark holder.

Table of Contents

Introduction

Many people in today's market have underestimated the power of the personal branding technique. There is a prevalent misconception that in order to achieve success in 2019 you have to be wildly exceptional and skilled beyond belief. However, every person has something unique to offer the world. The difference between whether they are successful or not lies not how skilled they are, and rather how well they package themselves and present their brands to the world. From Kim Kardashian to Martha Stewart, successful personal branding techniques have proven to be useful if not downright necessary to be a success today. Even for those who just wish to get a better job or specific opportunity, personal branding can still be used to set you apart from the crowd and better your efforts exponentially.

The following chapters will discuss proven tips

and techniques for getting the best mindset to undertake your new endeavor, as well as an in-depth history and explanation of personal branding and why it is important. You will also find checklists and step by step guides to follow as you build your personal brand, as well as information on how to curate and manage accounts across social media. Finally, you will also find helpful examples of personal brands all throughout the book, as well as information on finding and securing mentorships and how to monitor your overall progress and success.

Chapter One: What is Personal Branding?

Most of us have probably heard of the term 'personal branding' before, right? Whether it was on the news, in a job-seeking self-help book, or even around the water cooler, it seems as though more and more people are talking about having a personal brand. So, what exactly *is* it? And more pressingly, why is it important?

A personal brand is essentially when people market their careers and titles, as well as their personalities and personas, as brands. This may be a big concept to grasp easily because it seems a bit ridiculous. How can a person be a *brand?* Let us take a moment to understand what a brand is. In the traditional sense, a brand is a uniquely named, uniquely designed entity that is used to sell a product or a chain of products. Brands are used to sell products and make money by creating an atmosphere around their logo and name that is associated with the positive aspects of whatever it is that they are selling. For example, one major brand most of us know and love is Nike, a company that produces athletic shoes and clothing. They have created a signature logo that many of us can recognize on the spot. They place that logo on everything they make to create a cohesive line of products that are recognizable as their own, as well as recognizable to others once consumers purchase their products and wear them in public, making them appear more popular and thus selling more products. They endorse famous athletes to create not only a wider branding image but a more 'high-end' one. If the most talented athletes use their products, they *must* be top of the line, right? They also ensure that the celebrities they endorse maintain a certain image themselves, one of dedication, pride, and sportsmanship, steering clear of other athletes who may be more troublesome so as to not affect the overall brand's image.

All of these things are done to create an overall feeling and impression among consumers about the brand. This is evidenced when you simply ask an average person to describe the brand using a few words. The common descriptors you'll hear are words like sleek, innovative, top of the line, and performance enhancing. You may even have respondents tell you how cool the brand is because *this* athlete or *that* celebrity wears them! So. You may be asking yourself right about now, "Ok, but does all of this have to with *personal branding?*" Well, personal branding is essentially the same process of maintaining a public image to sell a product. Only the product isn't a new pair of shiny sneakers or fuzzy wristbands. The product is you and your career. YOU are the uniquely designed, uniquely named entity that is used to make money, and you do not have to be a celebrity to do it. Your personal brand is an impression held by someone other than yourself that describes the experience of you and your relationship to others. To understand why personal branding is so important, you first have to understand the history of the personal branding concept.

Since mankind was first created, we have had to interact with others. And since we have had to interact with others, we have had to watch what we say and how we present ourselves. As time has moved rapidly forward, in today's world we now more than ever have seemingly endless areas in which we have to cultivate our personalities and how we interact with other people.

We have to attend schools and playdates and extra-curricular activities when we are young. As adults, we have to show up to jobs, go shopping in stores, attend family functions, cultivate friendships, take part in hobbies, and navigate the seemingly endless journey to finding a spouse and raising a family. During all of these situations, we are interacting with others, and whether consciously or sub-consciously, are seeking to make an impression on those around us. Consider this for a moment. No matter where you are going, you take a dedicated amount of time to choose your clothes, prepare your hair and face, perhaps put on accessories. If you are an adult with any manners, you consider what you are going to say before you say it aloud. And depending on where you are and who you are with, you may choose to phrase your words differently or even not say what is really on your mind at all. This is because whether you would like to admit it or not, you want others to view you in a particular way. You may act very kind to others when among your church group, and yet when you are in the supermarket maybe your response to a rude shopper isn't always 'Peace be with you". Personal branding is very much just an extension of what we have been taught to do our entire lives. It is simply a more concentrated and researched effort to ensure that what others think of us is how we *want* them to think of us, and then utilizing that image for personal gain, whether it be financially, socially, or perhaps even both. Doing this does not make someone a sociopath or cold. It is simply recognizing, then using the good things we have to offer to share it with other people. Personal branding is *not* turning a monster into a prince. Rather it is turning a pauper into the prince he could always have been. The majority of people use their personal brand for good, to make people laugh online, sell genuinely innovative products, or endorse their careers to get better opportunities to do what they do best. Isn't that what we all want to do?

The concept of utilizing your personal brand and position to cultivate success was first introduced in 1937 by the author Napoleon Hill in his novel titled *Think and Grow Rich*. Since then, the idea that a person could simply market themselves to see the results and successes they wanted has appeared in countless books and informational guides. This may very well be due to the fact that the media is an essential tool to self-branding, and its use and progression has only increased dramatically over the years. During the 1940s, a person could create a brand only by becoming a prominent figure in society, whether it be an athlete, a politician, a film star, or a radio reporter. These people could quite easily control their personas in the media, as the only means by which people were connected were through radio, print, and small films. Scandals were few. News reports only focused on the important information of the day, so if a rising figure wanted their brand to shine or expand, they could take part in a magazine spread or newspaper interview. Another way that a person could increase their public image was by being asked to endorse a product, and getting placed in radio, billboard, or print ads for the product. When a celebrity endorsed a product during these times, the sales would increase greatly and that celebrity's image would hold strong as being relevant and cool, especially if their product was a new invention or viewed as being risqué.

During the 1950s, 60s, and 70s, the use of personal branding by prominent figures in society only increased with the popularization of television and subsequently television advertising. Politicians could run ad campaigns of themselves holding babies, rescuing animals, and fighting for justice for the people. Celebrities could participate in product advertising and even appear on shows meant to let them show off their personalities and positive qualities, such as game shows, talk shows, or variety shows. People could participate in interviews in media channels that were now far-reaching compared to the media of yesteryears and could reach wider audiences with their brands. Even professionals such as chefs, craftsman, and artists could create programming to not only show people how to create certain things but to also showcase their own unique brand of cooking or painting. Many of these professionals began their own line of supplies so that consumers could more closely mimic their techniques, or at the very least *feel* as if they could. Often, during this time period, those wanting to better increase their public image would publish auto-biographies, cookbooks, or how-to guides. It was also during this time that ordinary people began using personal branding within their own lives to achieve more success.

The 1950s was an era filled with new inventions

and products, as well as a time in many ways dedicated to maintaining the traditional ways of American life. A husband was expected to secure a good job that paid well, and a wife was expected to produce lots of children and maintain a clean household. Families were also expected to maintain a host of personal investments, such as new, shiny cars, washing machines, and microwave ovens. Keeping up with the Jones's was no longer a fad, it was a way of life. In order to appear well-off, stable, and modern to all of your friends and neighbors, the average woman was expected to wear the right clothes for her locale, have her hair be styled just so, and have a well-equipped household that was clean and orderly for her husband to come home to. Men were expected to act wholesome and support their families financially by purchasing the best of what was new. Everyone had to ensure they kept their conversations light and pleasant. All of these things were needed to be complete in order for a person to have a rich social life and be viewed with high regard in their communities.

When examined, the 1950s cultivated not just the idea of personal branding, but rather an entire culture based around the idea of presenting your best self to others and watching very closely how others regarded you. While during this decade personal branding on a daily basis was focused primarily on being just like everyone else, during the 1960s after the introduction of the counterculture movement, personal branding for most shifted to focusing on what made you unique.

During the 1980s, personal branding techniques became more on point than ever before. For the first time throughout history, self-help books became widely popular as people sought to improve themselves to become more successful. It was during this time, however, that many authors and individuals well-versed in personal success preached the idea that true success came not from self-improvement, but from self-packaging. Everyone has good and bad qualities, and while you can work to improve the negative aspects of your personality, ultimately people will still be people and will still have flaws. However, self-packaging will allow you to present *only* those qualities that are positive and use them to your advantage, creating a more genuine self-brand rather than pretending to be someone or something that you simply are not. The techniques provided by those well-versed in personal branding were utilized by businessmen, entrepreneurs, and professionals alike. It was also during the 1980s that the most important tool for self-branding was invented and marketed; the internet.

When it was first introduced to the public market, the internet was seen by many as a tool for technology geeks and those with less important things to do with their time. Even with the introduction of email, many people still preferred snail-mail to having to log onto a computer and learn a whole new program just to communicate with someone they could easily just call or write. However, as the technology of the internet and personal computers became ever quicker and more user-friendly, the popularization of computer technology for the average person continued to increase throughout the 1980s and 90s, and by the 2000s became a necessity for people to brand themselves personally. In order to be seen as a professional, you had to have a working email, resumes typed using word processing software, and computers that could be used to work on. You could even purchase more and more items online with Amazon or eBay in the 90s, and people could find useful information about you and your career on your website rather than in the phonebook.

The search engine Google was created in 1998, and within just a few years most people shifted to learning things online rather than in books or educational films. Questions could be answered with the push of a button, and similarly, people could find out what they wanted to know about you and your brand in a matter of seconds. 2004 brought the invention of an entirely new avenue for marketing and branding; Facebook. While Facebook was originally intended to be a social networking site to keep you in touch with friends and family, it quickly became a catalyst for people to create entire personas for themselves online. Facebook incited a wave of new media channels, including YouTube in 2005, Instagram in 2011, and Twitter in 2007.

Suddenly, you did not have to be a celebrity or politician or even have a career to have people pay attention to you. If you could create media that people would be interested in, you could become noteworthy. However, these channels quickly became flooded with people from all around the globe who could create interesting videos, posts, and other content for people to view. It quickly became difficult to stand out among the crowds, and this meant fewer opportunities for people to become noticed and for their personal brand to be recognized. This problem was alleviated, however, when content creators for such avenues began to seriously study social media market consumptions and began to focus on cultivating specific branding, marketing it to specific audiences. Once one creator began doing this, it became possible for others to follow suit and create a new portal for people to not only create an online presence but to actually begin to make money off of content. A creator could market a video on YouTube that could garner millions of views, resulting in thousands of dollars of revenue. On revenue free sites such as Facebook, Twitter, and Instagram, a person looking to expand their success opportunities could partner with a product brand and endorse it to make money if they had a large following. They could create their own product lines based off of what content they produced, and even simply sell merchandise with their faces on it. They could even create a personal brand highlighting their knowledge in a particular area of expertise, such as interior decorating, and use it to get a real-life job in the field.

Today, virtually every company has accepted that social media and online platforms are the avenues by which most people receive information and advertisements, and are moving their advertising marketing into those areas. Similarly, personal branding today takes place mostly online, with mainly celebrities or other public figures using other methods such as television or film to reach their audience.

Now that you have a great understanding of what personal branding looks like and how it has evolved until now, we can answer the question of *why* personal branding is important. If you want to be successful *financially*, you have to be able to be a *professional* success. In today's market, there are every day more and more qualified candidates flooding the job market for skilled positions, and even on platforms such as film, television, social media, and online forums, there is an ever-increasing amount of competition and content. The only way in which to stand a chance at securing a well-paying career in any field nowadays is to stand out to employers and audiences alike, providing them with what they want to hear and see. The only way to determine what they want is to *research* what they want and then figure out how to implement it into what you already have going for yourself. Regardless of the specifics of your audience, everyone wants to feel that, if they are paying a person to do a job or taking the time to watch that person, that person is someone unique, someone special, and is providing something that no one else on the market is providing. The only way to do this is to create a very personal, positive brand for yourself and your career, cultivating an image with awesome connotations and selling points.

Those who are unsuccessful at trying to become a musician, actor, YouTuber, a working professional engineer, professor, or even a lawyer is because they did not work on creating a personal brand for themselves. They were content to be just like everyone else, hoping their qualifications and skills would see them through to new opportunities. But there is a fatal flaw in this very common reasoning; ANYONE can match your qualifications. That prestigious university you went to? It didn't say "John Only" under its Latin insignia. The degree you worked for? Anyone with good enough credit for student loans or enough money saved already could have gotten that same degree anywhere in the country thanks to online schools. The skills you worked so hard for were not invented upon your learning them. Countless others had to learn them to achieve the same goals you did. Factor into this equation the very real fact that someone else, always, at any time, will have more experience than you. They may not be looking for the same job as you right now or be living in your area, but someday, they might. And if all you have to hold up to a potential employer or an audience of the world is the same thing they've already seen on someone else's resume or media accounts, you may as well write the phrase "YOU DON'T *NEED* ME" on your forehead. While you should obviously seek to be qualified in your area of career, you need to cultivate that 'je ne sais quoi' personality in order to get ahead and be the one that others look to for more guidance on how they too can become successful.

Ultimately, a personal brand is your best tool for success in 2019. Now that you understand what it is and how it is important, you can begin to work towards cultivating a unique personal brand of your own and take charge of your future!

Chapter Two: An Introduction to Personal Branding in 2019

As you now already know, personal branding in 2019 looks a lot different than personal branding even just twenty years ago. However, the most successful branding techniques from earlier years can still be relevant today; we just have to learn to apply them to newer platforms. In learning how a personal brand can begin successfully and evolve over time to meet the market demands, let us take an in-depth at one of the most influential personal brands of all time: Martha Stewart.

Martha Stewart began her career in 1976 when she created a small catering company with her friend and ran it out of her basement. From there, Martha was hired to manage gourmet food supply stores and continued to grow her catering company. While providing food for a book release party, she was introduced to an influential publisher at the time, who recognized her unique taste and ability to cook and decorate flawlessly. From there, he contracted her to write a cookbook focused on entertaining guests, and in 1982 Martha released her first cookbook entitled *Entertaining*. Within the next 10 years, she would go on to publish more than 10 cookbooks and lifestyle how-to guides, as well as appearing on countless television programs, such as *The Oprah Winfrey Show* and late-night talk shows. She also began writing dozens of articles for newspapers and magazines on homemaking and cooking, and in 1990 developed a lifestyle magazine called *Martha Stewart Living*. From there, Martha went on to create a 30-minute weekly television show in 1993, inviting viewers to create things featured in her magazine, and eventually launched her show to air new 60-minute episodes every day of the week in 1997. During this time she also appeared on *The Today Show* and *The Early Show* and appeared on several different magazine covers.

In 1997, Martha consolidated all of her business ventures under one brand, entitled *Martha Stewart Omnimedia*. She was able to use this company to secure greater ad times for her lines of products, her magazines, and even launched a business website and mail catalog. By 1999, Martha became the first self-made woman billionaire in U.S. history and continues to be one of the richest people in the United States.

Throughout her entire career, Martha has garnered astronomical opportunities for success and wealth. This was not achieved, however, because she was so much better than or talented than anyone else alive at the time. All her successes can be linked to the fact that, from the very beginning of her career, she carefully and meticulously curated a personal brand for her name and persona. She utilized her good qualities, like her knack for home-decorating and cooking and used them to curate a unique style for herself. The pictures featured in her books were elegant and tasteful, but unlike the traditional concepts people were accustomed to.

Her decorating styles incorporated themes from New England and yet were universal enough to be used throughout the country, setting her apart from more regional or more general professionals trying to make it in her field. Her recipes were designed to be easy for the home cook to understand, but used fine ingredients and were often meant to impress. Her demeanor was always one of cheer and class, while her wardrobe spoke of simplicity, cleanness, and elegance. She displayed her passion for helping others to entertain and impress by utilizing countless media avenues including print and television to give tutorials and tips for achieving decorations and food like her own. She then very smartly took control of her personal brand even more by consolidating all of her efforts into one company, and aptly gave that company her very own name. She even began a lifestyle magazine, so that others could literally try and achieve a Martha Stewart 'feel' in every aspect of their homemaking. Her personal brand became established as one of the most iconic facets of

Americana to date.

Another hallmark of her personal brand was its ability to weather her scandal in 2004. She was charged for insider trading in regards to her company and even spent time in prison. While this greatly contrasted with her 'goody-goody' homemaker image, she launched a re-branding effort in 2005 and actually began another television series that saw wonderful successes, and has continued to publish new cookbooks and lifestyle magazines in the years since. This is mainly due to the fact that, while people struggled to accept her wrong-doing, she *still* provided audiences and consumers with a style and brand that no other could match, because *no one else was Martha Stewart*. While others could have written a similar amount of cookbooks or been on television as much as she was, there was no replacement for her styling, demeanor, and face. Let us take a moment to consider the downfall of another famous cook and homemaker, Paula Dean. While her scandal centered on her use of a racial slur rather than fraudulent gain, one could look at her career and draw many comparisons between her and Martha. They both had successful product lines and were seemingly unique in their presentations. While Martha had a classy, elegant charm, Paula had a humble, down-home drawl. But when Paula's empire fell, there were already several qualified candidates to take her place. The Food network already had other cooks from the south producing shows, and it didn't take long for the shelves of stores like Wal-Mart to clear out their Paula Dean merchandise and replace it with the now beloved Pioneer Woman. However, when Martha was taken off the air, while there were certainly other lifestyle and cooking gurus out there, none could parallel her history and sense of style. At the end of the day, people are more willing to forgive those that they view as irreplaceable or necessary. While I am sure another Martha Stewart-esque icon could emerge in the future, they will not be successful until the original herself steps out of the spotlight.

Martha Stewart Living has continued to reach

millions of people by print and has kept up with the times by popularizing various apps associated with the Martha Stewart brand as well as e-letters and website updates. Martha began selling many years ago and to this day continues to sell a wide variety of products associated with cooking, crafting, and home décor, to everything from paper goods to rolling pins to yes, even food and pet supplies. All of her products feature a cohesive color scheme of pastel blue and white, signature colors of elegance and peacefulness. All of her products are available for purchase across her various platforms, and all carry on them her name.

Martha even maintains accounts across social media, using her platforms there to advertise her products and reaffirm her style, by posting pictures of elegant place settings she's created or new ideas she has had for entertaining. She even uses her accounts, such as Twitter, to advertise her partnerships with other companies, offering discounts on their websites with her special codes and telling of how wonderful she believes their products to be. She has even taken plenty of her financial resources and time to participate in a variety of non-profit campaigns and has a special heart for animals, contributing to their rescue and safekeeping. Martha has even created a show with Snoop-Dog to reach a wider audience merely based off of intrigue. *What on earth could a show featuring clean-cut Martha Stewart and street-tough rapper Snoop-Dog possibly be about?* People tune in to answer this very question, and Martha is all the richer because of it. Her various shows from years past are now available on streaming television sites, and her books are available as e-books to keep up with the technological advances of the times.

Ultimately, you can see how Martha's pattern of success lies in her business acumen and ability to curate a unique personal brand for herself and name. Throughout her 40 plus years in the industry, her name has become synonymous with warmth, class, elegance, and entertaining, and this was no accident. She used trigger words for just such things throughout every appearance and book and show she has ever made and has a seemingly endless collection of decorating and cooking segments dedicated to achieving such feelings in your own home. She actively participates in and seeks out paid partnerships with brands that connect to her lifestyle choices. She has utilized, without fail, the most far-reaching and innovative technologies of her day to spread her personal brand to audiences around the country and world. She has identified that while her particular brand will not speak to those in lower-income households or those without a care for interior decorating, she recognizes that *her* audience consists of middle class and upper-class women who want their homes to be pretty and parties to be remarkable. She does not change her ingredient list to cater to what she knows they sell at Wal-Mart and often calls on her followers and viewers to seek out the 'best quality' ingredients or craft supplies. She even makes and sells lines of high-end pet supplies because she is fully aware that members of her audience have money to spare on their pets.

How does her brand survive if it doesn't appeal to most people? It is the sheer fact that while many could not afford her lifestyle, it is the *promise and feelings* a glimpse of her lifestyle create in people. I will never cook a 5-course meal that serves pork tenderloin cutlets in a bolognaise sauce to 25 guests and ends with a line of croquembouches towers. But to watch her create such things makes me feel like someday maybe I could host a fancy party, and THAT is how she appeals to more and more people. And most of all, she does everything she does, all of this, unapologetically. She never claimed to be a woman of the working class family. She never claimed that her recipes would be easy for a working mother to make. All she has ever done is identified her niche market, sold the idea of finer living to even more people to expand her market, and has curated a well put together and elegant image that tells people *'You can trust me'*. Ultimately, Martha Stewart has created one of the most iconic personal brands for herself and has become a multi-billionaire, household name by simply working hard to package herself and everything she has to offer to the media and consumer alike.

Now that you have a firm grasp of what one example of a successful personal brand looks like, we can now begin to explore how personal branding can still lead to success in other areas and career fields. Not every successful personal brand has to become as famous as Martha Stewart or create multibillion-dollar companies and legacies. Average, everyday people can use the same techniques as the most successful and rich people in the world to greatly improve their own lives and cultivate a personal brand for themselves, and understand why doing so is essential to get ahead of the game.

You can even curate a personal brand for yourself for personal reasons. While most people are content to allow their personalities to speak for themselves, often you'll find that the most socially and personally successful people- those with great friends and familial relationships, as well as large followings online- take the time and effort to simply fine tune what they already have going for them. They create well-manicured social accounts that all have a set color scheme and theme. They wear clothing all of a similar style and put on makeup or style their hair regularly. They make the extra effort to control or alleviate their negative qualities and when interacting with others, they ensure they have a good sense of humor and are kind and thoughtful. While this may seem unnecessary to iterate, very few people actually take the time to put a *concentrated effort* into being a good person. Most people tend to think that it will just happen naturally, and if it doesn't, it just wasn't meant to be. However, that notion simply isn't true. We all have good qualities that could make us great people and give us a rewarding social life and reputation if we merely took the time and thought into ensuring we let those qualities and habits shine in our everyday conversations and interactions. Your personal brand is simply YOU, only operating on a clearer frequency and sent in a more palatable package. It lets people know that you care about yourself, and so they should care about you too. Why can't you use the idea of personal branding to implement positive change in every aspect of your life, not just your professional career?

In today's ever increasingly competitive job market, even if you have the skills or education to qualify you for a particular position, employers are now starting to seek out candidates that will not only meet the job expectations but exceed them outside of the workplace. In years past, one could simply print out a resume, set up an interview, and be on the fast track towards securing a coveted position. However, with the use of social media and online marketing techniques skyrocketing in recent years, more employers are choosing to vet applicants online. They will search for your social accounts and see what kind of content you share and follow. They will see if you have any documented experience in the area listed in your profiles on sites such as LinkedIn. They want to see some evidence of your online literacy. While you could have the same or even a superior resume to another applicant, your social accounts could be what sinks you in the running for a position. This is why the idea of personal branding is so important. While Facebook and other sites may have been created with the idea that content would only be shared with people you know in real life, they have now become likened to a dating profile. People understand that the information you provide is supposed highlight your good qualities and beliefs, and these platforms are no longer a place to act comfortably or only put in a half-effort.

Instead, you should take the time to curate each of your accounts to match the best version of yourself that you could be. The internet also has places where you could post blogs or contribute content to organizations that could be associated with your career fields, such as marketing, finance, or even sites for teachers, artists, or trades. If you are able to create an online presence, you not only improve your chances at getting a coveted position or advancing in your field, but you also create more leverage and legitimacy for your personal brand to add to your resume and profile. You can also partner with others in your field to establish connections and perhaps provide a potential employer with an informed reference or mentor who could attest to your personal brand and it's worth and value.

Personal branding is also very important even if you are your own boss and hiring officer. Over 85% of available career paths involve some degree of customer service, and consumers want to see a personal brand just as much as potential employers do. If you are able to market your company successfully, that is wonderful. But sooner or later, you will have to increase your edge over competitors. This can be achieved by adding your *personal* brand to your professional one if you haven't already done so. Clients love to know with whom they are doing business and giving money to, and so if you are able to package yourself as a dedicated, passionate professional in your field with unique features a, b, and c, people will choose to come to your business over a competitor. Seeing a smiling face and genuine persona means more than people realize, and while it may seem old-fashioned, it truly is what can set you apart from others in today's marketplace. In the following chapters you will learn the specifics of how to create a personal brand by learning how to achieve the best mindset for the task, creating a custom to-do list, how to define your audience, how to curate your accounts across four different social media platforms, and how to seek out mentors and monitor your progress.

Chapter Three: Having the _RIGHT_ Mentality to Buila Personal Brand

Building a personal brand can be a very rough business. It involves a great deal of hard work and dedication, and it can take an extended period of time before you begin to see the results you would like to. This entire process can and will become all the more frustrating if you are not in the right place mentally to undertake it. A personal brand is designed to make you marketable and attractive to consumers, which will mean opening yourself up to the judgment and scorn of the public eye. People who intend to make a profit off of their personal brands online such as Instagram gurus or YouTube stars are constantly bombarded with personal attacks from strangers. You may even be reprimanded by others genuinely trying to help you along in the process, such as by a mentor or consultant. They are there to tell you things that you may not be able to see clearly for yourself and offer an outside opinion. While it is important to remember to stay true to yourself, the input of others is a valuable and crucial resource to the building of your personal brand, and you must be willing to accept constructive feedback as well as be able to ignore hateful comments from those you are not seeking advice from. This is why having the right attitude is important as you begin the process of building your personal brand, and following are some helpful guidelines to implement along the way.

- Be positive.

When it comes to building a personal brand, consumers and viewers alike are attracted to positive people. There is no use in trying to become someone or something that you are not, so if you attempt to build a personal brand with only the veneer or appearance of having a positive attitude, then you will be sorely disappointed when you do not yield positive results. There is a lot to be said about social intuition, and many people are able to identify when others are not being genuine. A positive persona makes people feel uplifted, safe, and as if they are able to more easily relate to you personally. Being a positive person means believing in yourself and trusting that you can accomplish the things you set out to. Having a positive mentality and way about you also means that you will be able to find more fulfillment in your work and results.

You may be asking yourself, "Ok, General. So what does having a positive attitude *actually* mean and look like?" Well, while a lot of people are able to try and be positive about the larger, life-changing situations we face, people often forget that the best way to transform positive *thoughts* into *positive attitudes* is the frequency of our positivity. The best way to begin building a positive attitude is to adjust your thought process on a daily basis. No matter what point you are at currently in your life, you can begin by waking up every day and recounting one thing you are thankful for that day. It may be something small, but being thankful is a positive quality that will help you feel better about your situation. Throughout your day, when you face problem people or problem situations, you can attempt to find at least one more good aspect than bad. For example, if you have a boss or coworker that is grinding on your last nerve, simply look at them and identify what it is about them that drives you crazy. Ok. They are bossy, disrespectful, and arrogant. Now look at them and find four things you *do* like about them. They are knowledgeable, dedicated, reasonable, and humorous. This may seem to be such a small change, but if every person just took the time to identify the good that exists in this world along with the bad, imagine where we would be right now. At the very least, *you* will be one step further to changing yourself for the better.

Once you have made the effort to try and change your thoughts for the better, you can try extending that positivity towards others. We have all heard the phrase 'fake it until you make it'.

That can mean a few different things to people, but the best way I have ever heard it explained is this; if you begin to act like the person you want to be, you will find it easier and easier to behave that way until you actually become that person. Behavior modification is an ongoing process, not an overnight decision. While you may have plenty of positive qualities, none of them will matter until you have the positive attitude needed to bring them to fruition in regards to personal branding. When you have a conversation with others, listen more than you speak. Smile, and try your best to genuinely care about them and what they are going through. When someone comes to you with difficulties, sympathize with their situation and do your best to provide them with a solution and support. Being a positive person in your personal life will make it substantially easier to allow that positive energy to shine through when you go to inject it into your personal branding efforts.

The common consensus is that it takes 30 days to make or break a habit. So make the conviction that having a positive thought process will be the habit you form this month. Have at least two positive interactions with others on a daily basis, and reiterate to yourself the reasons why you want to be a positive person. DO NOT allow those reasons to be money motivated or else you will fail. A good reason would be that having a positive attitude will help you to appreciate your life and success more wholeheartedly. Or perhaps it could be that you want to become more genuinely likable to others. Your reasoning should never be that you want to market your personal brand successfully and this book told you that you needed to have a positive attitude to do so. You absolutely do need a positive attitude to do so. But you need to be able to find your own, personal reason for wanting to have such an attitude in the first place, even if that reason is simply that you know you have good qualities and you don't want to see them wasted because of your negative attitude. A genuine reason you have in your heart is better than a thousand reasons you simply think are the right answer.

- Be dedicated.

Building a personal brand is going to take a lot of time and effort. You will need to take many hours to curate your social media pages and then even more hours to keep them up. You will need to invest more time and perhaps even finances into choosing the correct wardrobe and styling for your brand and work to maintain your appearance daily. You will most likely need to put some sleepless nights under your belt in order to create content and even learn new skills if you decide to try and market your personal brand online for profit. All of these things will become overwhelming if you do not have the work ethic and dedication to see them through. One great way to become more dedicated to what you are doing is to make a schedule to incorporate your goals and tasks into your daily routine. Yes, having a schedule will keep you organized and you will be better off in the long run for having done it. But you would be surprised how much easier accomplishing tasks seems and how much more excited you could be when it comes to your work when you have predestined times set aside to work. The to-do list you create won't seem as daunting and you will be far less likely to procrastinate if you feel that you can reasonably accomplish things ahead of time.

Being evicted to building your personal brand also means that you will have to dedicate time and focus to consistency. Your brand will not much of a brand at all if your media accounts, content, resumes, profiles, products, and words don't have a cohesive ascetic and theme. In order to be a unique entity, you must be an entity, not a random hodge-podge of things. This also means ensuring your personal look and appearance remain constant, and your demeanor remains consistent as well. No one looks at Martha Stewart and says "She's a very well-put-together woman except for those few times she went on Oprah in her pajamas...". It will be easier for you practice consistency with yourself from the start so that when you do begin to experience success, it won't become overwhelming to suddenly feel as if you have to rush to 'keep up' appearances or content. A dedication to your brand and consistency in your work is the firm foundation on which you will build your empire.

- Be passionate.

You are going to be trying to sell the idea of YOU. And no one will want to buy what you are selling if they do not believe you are truly passionate about whatever it is you are doing. Having a passion for your work, even if that work is simply self-branding on social media, will be the fuel behind the fire of how dedicated you are in the long run. If you are not passionate about your work, it will be substantially harder to find the motivation to put the effort into working hard and making the time to curate your personal brand. Some say that when you are truly passionate about what you do, you never work a day in your life. However, even those that love the work that they do still feel as if they are working some days. Every effort a person sets out to pursue will involve some tasks that they may not enjoy. The more involved you become in your work and the more responsibility you take on in your branding efforts, the more of those kinds of tasks you will have to take on. They may become monotonous or overwhelming, even leading you to quit your efforts, if you do not have the areas you are truly passionate about to look forward to. A strong passion will lead you through the more difficult or seemingly never-ending trials you will have to face on the road to success, and will give you hope and drive to continue forward.

Having the passion for your work and career will also help you to a better home in your skills and knowledge in your field. While some areas may not require a full college degree in order to be knowledgeable or well trained, every single career path requires some amount of study and know how in order to improve and move on to better opportunities. While on the job training is bound to happen as most people learn best when in the thick of their work, many opportunities will greatly benefit from taking the extra step and making the time to learn more about your field and career through research outside of your workday. This could mean reading books or articles published by those who became successful in your area detailing how you too, can find success. You could conduct online research and find valuable information that will help you achieve your goals or fix a common problem you see happening in your profession. Broadening you working knowledge of, well, your work, could even mean working extra hours from home or testing new theories on your own time. Whatever gaining more knowledge in your field looks like to you, if you want to covet better opportunities for yourself and get ahead of your competitors, you will have to gain this knowledge outside of your average workday. It will seem downright impossible to dedicate any of your personal time to learning more about something if you aren't passionate about that something.

- Be focused.

There will be many distractions throughout your journey to build a profitable personal brand.

These things can include personal issues and goals, familial situations, or perhaps just the obligations involved in maintaining a household and adult life. There will always be bills to pay, mouths to feed, relationships that need your attention. It is important to maintain a balance between your personal life and professional one, as a life solely dedicated to either facet of yourself will ultimately leave you feeling incomplete. However, one of the unique features of marketing a personal brand is that everything you do IS personal, and you need to have a strong sense of yourself in your personal life in order to succeed in your professional marketing of yourself. Accomplishing any goal in life will require a very large amount of focus, however building a personal brand will ultimately require not only focusing on your professional attributes and skills but also focusing on your unique personal contributions and traits and tailoring them to your desired style. Building a successful personal brand will require a near constant observation of and content creation for your various social media accounts, blogs, and channels. You will have to be focused on your appearance and demeanor when presenting yourself to the world and carefully monitor your behavior to achieve the results you desire. Maintaining this degree of focus may at times prove difficult, but is absolutely necessary to remain in control of your personal brand and curate for yourself the persona you wish to market.

- Be willing to ask for input.

Your personal brand is meant to be marketed to other people, right? So how exactly will you know what others think or feel about you and your personal brand if you do not prepare yourself to ask them? When you have a specific vision or plan in mind for your image and persona, it can be difficult to humble yourself and ask for the opinions of others. But you must be in a mindset where you are willing to accept and even seek out the input of others in order to succeed. While not every thought or suggestion from an outside source should be implemented in your brand, it is important to recognize that good feedback and help can come from anywhere and anyone. Acknowledging this and subsequently seeking out feedback will require you to be in a strong enough place within yourself so that you are able to stay true to who you are without being so rigid that you become off-putting to others.

To accomplish this balanced mindset, you need to acknowledge a few things. Firstly, you are uniquely talented and what makes you marketable is non-negotiable. Secondly, you also have to remember that other people will always be able to see a flaw, a consequence of action, or even a positive attribute you are unable to see clearly for yourself. Thirdly, you must know your resource in order to be able to correctly judge the value of their input. A random stranger's word may be taken with a stronger grain of salt than that of your experienced mentor, for example. You should also take a moment to not only gauge the qualifications and experience of your resource but also their motives. What would they have to gain or lose by giving you the input they are giving? More often than not you will find a person's only objective is to help you succeed, allowing you to more easily trust the feedback others are giving you rather than jumping on the feeling of being personally attacked or undermined. Being humble and yet astute and grounded enough to accept and implement the opinions and thoughts of others requires walking a very fine line and balance, but can be achieved so long as you begin your process of building a personal brand with the intention to accomplish these things in your personal mindset and behavior towards others.

- Be sure of who you are.

While we will discuss later on the in-depth process of remaining true to who you are and why it is so important *during* the building of your brand, it is valuable to keep in mind *before* building a brand as well. When you first come to the decision that you want to build a brand, you may have an idea of what that will look like.

Scenes may come to mind of perfectly coordinated social media pages, a large following on digital streaming channels, and perhaps getting to endorse products or appear in print or television. You may even imagine a less public personal brand wherein you have a great and unique reputation with employers and coworkers alike, or even just among friends and family. No matter what your vision for your own personal brand is centered on, I'm sure the most central factor in your equation was *you*. It would be near impossible for someone with no self-esteem or personal value to decide that they and their personalities were worth marketing. Before the process even began, and all you had was thought to build a personal brand and decided to purchase this book, you could see the amazing and unique qualities that made you think "I can do this!".

You had a voice you knew no one else could mimic and a career or persona that could appeal to an audience. This feeling is the key to being successful as a personal brand and is truly the only way to achieve the goals that you will be setting for yourself and working towards. The world, your audience, your friends and family and mentors, will all be telling you which way to lean and what to wear and how to act. Their input is valuable, but at the end of the day, the only one who has to live with the choices you make is you. Being sure of who you are as a person and what you have to offer is the only way to ensure you will be happy and achieved in this line of work and marketing. Being sure of who you are will perhaps also help you to maintain a grounded moral compass and humility throughout the ups and downs of your career. Once you begin seeing some successes, it could be quite easy if not downright human to begin to feel prideful and full of all your glory. I mean, you are a success, so why can't you feel like you're one, right? However, this type of mindset will always seep into how you behave and speak, and especially if your brand is based in media creation or heavily relies on your persona, you can quickly become off-putting and sink your rising ship. No one from any demographic or audience wants to see a jerk who thinks they're 'all that' try and relate to them, and being arrogant is just a short road to nowhere.

Knowing who you are and where you come from can help you keep you grounded amongst the work that you do, and can also be a source of hope for you if your career and brand face turbulent trials. You will be sure to remember that you still have something to offer no matter where you are at in your journey, and that is a comfort too many forget to utilize. Just take a look at the most well-liked public figures in 2019. Jennifer Lawrence is noted as being one of the most humble and humorous actresses today and did not get that reputation by acting better than those around her. Instead, she makes an effort to make jokes and be a warm presence to coworkers and interviewers alike, never taking herself or her fame seriously at all. She makes a clear point to the world that she loves her work, but not only does not seek fame but rather dislikes that aspect of her work. This quality is what makes her all the more likable to fans and companies looking to hire her, and if you employ a similar attitude and mindset you are sure to be much better off in the long run of your efforts. In contrast, you could examine the low likability of other personal brands due to a dissimilar attitude, such as Kanye West. While we won't be discussing his exploits or opinions that have rocked his image, one defining facet of why many dislike him today is that he has no problem talking about his fame and why he is so deserving of it, even deciding on multiple occasions to talk about how amazing he is. While he will always have diehard fans who respect his honesty and even those who dislike him personally may still enjoy his music, he will always be a divisive and controversial brand, turning off many people and ultimately closing the door on opportunities for his career. While money and success may be of no concern to Kanye anymore, YOU still have to consider those things for yourself and your brand. Do you really want to jeopardize everything you worked for so that you can take a public victory lap? People love humble people who seek to uplift others and be a positive presence for all, not just themselves.

- Be purposeful in everything you do.

Finally, you must be purposeful in everything that you do. Basically, this just means that you cannot simply make a career-defining decision without ensuring your every action in this move and all others is purposefully set up to help you achieve your goals in your personal brand. Every picture you post, every video you create, every outfit you style, every interview or blog post you participate in. Every book you read, every class you take, they should all be in service to building your personal brand. Nothing will come out of your action if you do not make it a purposeful action. Making decisions based on purpose and drive will help you to make the most of your decisions and time. Essentially, if every action has a purpose, then o action is wasted. Every action is in service to you and your career, and this mindset will help you further convict you towards your ultimate end game. Do you want to become a YouTube star or Instagram guru? Do you want to land life-changing job offers in your field or create a recognizable brand for your persona? These goals will require a lot of hard work along the way, and to make the most out of your work you will need to make decisions and budget your time with purpose. Even small decisions, such as which color of eyeshadow you wear or what kind of lighting you have in your picture will have an impact on your brand. So make these decisions with purpose and you will see the results you are looking for rather than the results circumstance makes for you.

Ultimately, you will need to keep all of these important things in mind when you first begin to build a personal brand, as well as maintain them and integrate them into your mindset throughout the process going forward. Building a personal brand can be grueling and scary and open you up to a lot of things in life, so it is essential and greatly important that you strive to have the right mindset to accomplish the task and find success. You will need to be a positive person and keep positive thought processes going even in the face of difficulty and setback. You will need to ensure you are dedicated to what you are doing and put the time and effort into your work. Passion will be a key factor in whether or not people invite your personal brand into their lives and whether you are happy and fulfilled when working towards your goals. Having a focused mind will help you to better utilize your time and get a clearer picture of what you want to achieve. Valuing the input of others will assist you in fine-tuning your personal brand to a wider audience and help you to greater capitalize on what you are marketing. Being sure of who you are as a person and what you have to offer the world will ensure you stay grounded and likable throughout the highs and lows of your brand's success and trials. Finally, being purposeful in everything you do will ensure your efforts are utilized as well as they possibly can be and the future and public imaging of your brand stay in *your* control, not the control of circumstance. If you work to implement these key pieces of advice into who you are as a person and how you react during your journey, you will surely see much more goals achieved than you previously would have and it could quite literally be the difference between success and failure for you and your brand at every stage.

Chapter Four: How to Build a Personal Brand

Now that you understand what personal branding is and what kind of mindset you need to have in order to do it, it is finally time to begin working on building the foundation for your personal brand. This foundational work will be what you build upon as time goes on, and will truly make the difference for you and your personal brand in the long run. Building a personal brand is vitally important if you wish to achieve long-term success in a career that is fueled by being in the public eye or is contingent upon having a reputation with others. Basically, personal branding is essential for most professionals, although it is rarely employed, giving *you* the upper hand in the market for deciding to undertake this journey. This chapter will be divided into two separate sections; what you will need to *have* in order to build a personal brand, and what you will need to *do* in order to build a personal brand. First, let us take a look at the checklist for what you will need to have to begin laying your foundation.

Much like building a house, building a personal brand does not happen overnight. Both involve a great deal of preparation work and planning, both mentally, emotionally, physically, and financially. Once you have prepared yourself for the massive undertaking, you then need to gather the materials necessary for the task at hand before pouring the foundation. Imagine the following checklist as your 'shopping list' for building your personal brand.

Personal Brand Shopping List: What do I need to start building my brand?

o Technology

This is quite literally the first material possession you will need to secure before building your personal brand. While not everyone can afford the brand new, top of the line Mac, it is important to understand the value and vital role that technology now plays in personal branding in 2019. Today, no matter what level of personal branding you wish to achieve, from online stardom to simply securing better job offers, some level of your personal branding will have to be conducted online. No matter what type of personal branding you wish to work towards, you must have a smart device, such as cell phone or tablet that you can carry with you throughout the day and on which you can download the latest apps for social networking. This device should also be connected to a data plan so that you can access your accounts without needing to connect to Wi-Fi.

It may even be beneficial to purchase a spate device on which you could conduct branding business and keep another device for personal use. This is mainly due to the problem or proper device storage. Many modern-day devices now have slots for SIM cards, which are basically small micro-discs you insert into your device to store pictures, videos, and apps on. Once these cards are full, however, you must remove them and insert a new card, which means you no longer have access to all of the things you placed on your old card. While you can change them out regularly, this can become frustrating and a hassle to many people. While your personal social media accounts will be used to build your personal brand, many people still use their phones to store pictures they do not intend to post to social media and apps that they simply use for their personal entertainment, such as games or content players. These apps and games combined with your professional ones can take up a great deal of your device's storage and may very well slow down the efficiency of your connections. So if you can afford the investment, you should seriously consider purchasing a separate smart device so you can keep professional pictures, videos, and apps clear from your other content allowing you better focus and utilization of your limited resources. An inexpensive tablet, for example, could be a great tool to use for such a purpose.

However, there are many people that even maintain a separate smartphone, solely due to the fact that it has all of the capabilities of a tablet, but is also capable of calling and texting. This means you can have a separate work line to answer inquiries for your personal brand without compromising your privacy and still being able to separate out your personal from professional content. Many major chain stores now sell pre-paid smartphones for substantially cheaper rates than contract carriers, which means you could, in theory, spend as little as $150 average to set up and $30 average monthly to maintain a separate smartphone, capable of everything your current phone is. This may even be a more affordable option than purchasing an expensive tablet and data plan. However, if this route still sounds more appealing to you, you could try investing in a number adding service. For a small fee, one of many different companies you chose from will connect your cell phone to two separate numbers and will allow you to answer both inconspicuously, without the caller or texter being notified that they are calling only one phone. This will help you to compartmentalize between your work and professional lives without compromising your privacy or purchasing and maintaining another cell phone.

Once you have your mobile devices and data plans set up, you will also need to ensure you have a desktop or laptop computer to conduct essentials on. While mobile devices are essential for social media, laptop or desktop computers are still necessary for many websites and programs to properly function, such as word processors and video editing software. These products by no means have to be top of the line, as even the lower cost options will still work well. However, it is important to remember that this technology is an investment, and the more work you intend to accomplish on this device, the harder it will be as time goes on if your device is of a lesser quality. If your ultimate goal is simply to curate a personal brand to get better job offers or personal enrichment, then your current laptop or desktop will be just fine. However, if your goal is to rely heavily on technologies to become a YouTube star or eventually run an entire multi-faceted company, then higher quality is best.

On that note, what path you wish to take will also determine what extra technology you purchase from here. YouTube stars often purchase professional portable cameras, microphones, and tripods. They also purchase video editing software programs and other things of that nature which we will discuss further in the book. Anyone seeking social media branding typically purchases lighting equipment. Those who wish to curate brands based off of a particular skill or already somewhat successful career will purchase faster processing computers so as to become bloggers or online experts. Even professionals such as chefs utilize technologies in their trades, such instant-read thermometers or subscriptions to food magazines. Basically, while you may not be entrenched in the process of building your personal quite yet, you need to remember to budget and plan for purchasing these extra technologies and understand the value of investing in them.

o Mindset

We discussed earlier the importance of having a positive mindset for undertaking your goal of personal branding, and you now understand why it is so important. That is why you should include it on your list of things to ensure you have before beginning to work towards building your brand. You need to remember to remain positive and dedicated, and while a mindset is not something you can purchase in the store, it is highly valuable none the less.

o Knowledge

The know-how for your chosen career field is not

something you can simply buy online or get from being able to say you have a degree. However, it is something that will require a great deal of time, and quite possibly money. Let us say for example that you desperately want to be a YouTube star. While you may be able to invest in the technology necessary for that undertaking, you will also have to invest your time and rain power into researching audiences, demographics, and successful techniques that others have used to become successful. You will also have to research how to use video software and technologies, as well as a variety of things when creating content for new topics and subjects. If your goal is to use your personal brand to become a famous chef, you will need to research the science behind cooking and why foods do the things that they do, why certain techniques work and others don't, and what type of problems your fans can expect to run into when recreating your recipes so they can avoid them in the first place. If your goal is to become an expert engineer and uniquely qualified in your field, while a personal brand will help you to become invaluable and set you apart, yes, you will still have to invest in getting a degree. No amount of personal branding can cover up a severe knowledge gap no matter where you are working, and people will eventually see through your branding techniques if there is nothing to substantiate them. Before you begin a personal branding effort, you have to be knowledgeable in your area. Personal branding is about marketing what you already have going for you, not smoke and mirrors techniques to help you gloss over the hard work necessary for success.

o Body

Yes, this is the oddest sounding requirement in the world. Why on earth would you need the right *body* to start building a personal brand? Well, while we would all like to believe that our society is one of love and not judgment, most of us know all too well that that is simply not true. There are certainly people of all shapes and sizes who have built successful brands, however, you simply have to be aware of how your physicality will factor into your brand, and if it does not convey the image you want, then you need to review your options for changing it. THIS DOES NOT MEAN PLASTIC SURGERY! Too often people get bogged down in this idea because the idea of a presenting your real self when you have flaws is somehow more daunting than the idea of embracing those flaws or working to soften them in other ways. In reality, addressing your physical appearance and how it affects your brand is actually quite simple. You merely need to have an adult conversation with yourself and be honest about how your brand may be affected or shaped by all of the different components of your physical appearance, including your hair, makeup, wardrobe, and body type. If you are a larger person and the brand you would like to build is focused on fashion, then you should consider tailoring your clothing choices to brands that cater to people of your size and celebrate body diversity. Research companies that may want to partner with you and open the door for new opportunities. Also, prepare yourself for the trials you may face in the public eye, but remember that knowing who you are and your value is vital to overcoming these hurdles. Your physical shape does not have to change in order to achieve your goals, you just have to be aware of how they will affect your results and plan accordingly.

If your personal brand is unaffected by your physical body shape, as many brands would be, then it is also important to remember the other aspects of your physical appearance and what message they convey to the world about you and your brand. If you wish to build a blog and personal brand around natural dieting and cooking, then your clothing choices could reflect that by employing natural color schemes and fabric patterns. Perhaps you could research bohemian style guides and looks. You could style your hair and makeup very little so as to downplay any artificial connotations associated with things like heavy makeup looks and hair-dos. If you wish to brand yourself as an ambitious entrepreneur, you could curate your look to include nice suits and few but expensive accessories and a clean haircut and shaven face. Even if these steps don't reflect the style you yourself currently have, there is an ideology called 'wear-apy', wherein you wear clothes that will make you feel a certain way. People change their aesthetic all the time, and you are no freak or fraud for doing the same. If you decide your brand would benefit from you wearing a certain style of clothing and you like doing so, then invest in these looks and eventually they will become a part of who you are and who you present yourself to be. Perhaps wearing these new clothes and styling your countenance differently will even help you to feel more successful and comfortable with the new role you are taking on.

It is important to remember, however, that any change you make to your appearance should be in service to your ultimate goal and desired aesthetic, but should absolutely be a natural extension of who you are as a person and what your special qualities reflect. While we touched on the importance of being genuine earlier and will go more in-depth on the subject later on, your appearance should never make you feel uncomfortable or like a costume, unless of course your brand is somehow built around the playing of a character, such as being a cosplay figure or designer. It will seem absolutely fake and fraudulent of you to take on an entirely different persona and look than what you currently have, but if the qualities you are capitalizing on are a genuine part of who you are as a person, then the physical reflection of those qualities should not appear completely out of the ordinary for you to take hold of.

o   Social Skills.

If you are an adult who has trouble interacting with others, it is not too late for you to learn how to be sociable. While the vast majority of people have a group of friends, colleagues, or relatives they are most comfortable with and can't talk to easily, many adults today struggle when meeting new people and can feel uncomfortable in heavy social situations. If you are deciding to take on the task of building your own personal brand, however, then you have to be able to overcome your fears and anxieties. While every successful personal brand is different and the positive qualities the person possess vary greatly, the common skill that every personal brand must have is an ability to talk openly and comfortably with others. Not all of us were born with the gift of gab, but everyone can gain it if they are willing to put in the hard work.

Working on your social skills is like pouring fresh chum into shark-infested waters without a lifeboat. Yes, it will seem that scary, because the only way to unlock that door around your mouth and mind is to immerse yourself in difficult social situations and force yourself to talk to other people. Take some time out of each day and find at least two new people to talk with. Approach them first, introduce yourself, and begin talking to them about something relevant. If the conversation goes well, keep it going until you find that one of you has to leave. Do this for two weeks straight, and then work on finding more stressful situations, such as a party or get together. Attend it solo and make a determined effort to talk to every new person you can. The more you talk with a person the more comfortable you become with them, so while it will feel excruciating and awkward, find another new person to talk to after a short time. When you build a personal brand, you have to learn how to be consistent in the delivery of your personality and dialect, no matter what situation you are in or with whom you are speaking. This means you have to behave the same way in your videos, pictures, interviews, and daily conversations.

Even if your lone purpose in personal branding is to secure better job opportunity, you will have to be consistent when talking with one potential employer to the next and maintain that demeanor and report once you start working. This is yet another reason why it is so important for you to be yourself; you cannot be a fake person every day for the rest of your career. You may as well be yourself from day one. Developing your social skills may take a long period of time before you finally feel one hundred percent comfortable with every situation, but so long as you begin actively working on improving them before you begin setting up your personal brand, you should be able to interact with others well as needed during the process of pouring your foundation. You will know you have succeeded when you can talk with others easily in most any situation. You will hopefully begin to realize that, just as you found you had small things in common with strangers, you will certainly have something in common with virtually anyone you meet.

Now you have the technology you will need to set up the foundation of your personal brand, as well as the knowledge, mindset, and physicality to lay the groundwork for your goals. When you have developed social skills, you are able to talk with people off from all walks of life and appeal to a wider audience. This means you can now begin the process of actually setting up your brand and getting just that much closer to establishing yourself as a force to be reckoned with in the marketplace and find the success you deserve.

Step by Step Guide for Beginning to Build Your Personal Brand

- Identify what you have to offer and where your value will lie.

We all have qualities that make us unique, and each of us has a special something that makes others want to get to know us. Perhaps you have a winning smile or a great sense of humor. Maybe you're able to see things that others can't and give great advice on the subject. These positive aspects of your personality will be the things you will focus on going forward in the process of your personal brand. After all, personal branding has been described as selling the idea of a relationship with you to other people. So sell them the best experience possible. If you are having trouble identifying your best qualities, it would be a perfect opportunity to begin to enlist the help of those who know you best. Ask your friends and family what it is about you that they enjoy most. Take a sampling of several different people to ensure that the results of your test are not biased or hyperbolic due to one person's input. While your entire list should not be comprised solely of what others tell you, getting to hear what other people see in you may help to act as a catalyst for your own discovery of what you like about yourself. This is not the time to focus on your flaws and how to improve them. Rather this is the time to focus on the things that are great about your personality and work to increase them and package them as an essential, irrevocable part of who you are.

Your good qualities do not have to only be things about your personality. You could incorporate many good things about yourself from different areas of your life. Everything has some value in what you bring to the table when you decide to pursue a personal brand for yourself. For example, you could have a great knack for wardrobe styling and color coordination. Perhaps you could have a superior knack for tech or programming. These are what I like to call 'ancillary attributes'. They are not the main personality traits that you will be packaging in your personal brand and marketing, nor are they the *main* skill, career, or trade that you will be capitalizing on. They are smaller, less pronounced but still significant skills that you have that may very well help you along the way. Even if you decide your main endeavor is to become an acclaimed cookbook author, having a great sense of technology could help you to explore new and innovative avenues to deliver recipes and create content for food lovers around the globe. If you are talented with color schemes and décor but your primary goal is to be a YouTube vlogger, perhaps you could create some videos based around your work in interior design and even write blogs or articles on the subject. Basically, the best kind of success stories is of renaissance personas, i.e. people who do lots of things well instead of only one thing very well.

Once you have determined your positive personality traits and your ancillary skillset, it is now time to find your primary selling point. Perhaps you have a skill with cooking, fashion, music, design, art, or comedy. Perhaps you are passionate about a specific cause or lifestyle. Maybe your main selling point is simply a package of all the things that make you relatable and interesting. Whatever this primary skill is, even if it is simply your personality, you can absolutely use it to create an influential and remarkable personal brand. It may require a great amount thought in order to narrow down your list of traits and skills, as people can have many interests but should primarily focus on one main venture, especially when first starting their personal brand. You want to become a renaissance persona, but not to pursue so many avenues at the same time that none of them can succeed.

Kim Kardashian was simply famous for being *Kim Kardashian* for years before she actually did something, capitalizing solely off her name and brand persona. Martha Stewart did not begin television shows, websites, apps, and magazines at the same time she began her cookbooks. She started with what she knew best and understood what her main objective was. Martha then built upon that foundation of success to build an even better and stronger personal brand, always ensuring to incorporate what she was known best for, her cooking and décor skills, into every new venture she pursued. An eclectic brand foundation is a weak brand foundation, and will not be strong enough to hold up the house you build upon it. You will always be able to use the best of what you have to offer, just perhaps not in a primary way initially. If you have a lot of great or positive qualities and skills, you could come up with several possibilities for your primary selling point, however, during the next steps in the process you MUST narrow it down to one. Below is a possible example of what your qualities list could look like.

Personality Traits

- *Funny, mom said I am always making her laugh with jokes. A coworker said that I crack him up at our lunch break. A sense of humor is sarcastic, observational. Tend to poke fun at others without hurting feelings or going too far. Spouse says I make the most jokes about myself when in private.*

- *Informed, always researching current events and both sides of political arguments, can repeat that information back to others and am passionate about doing so, can process information and incorporate historical, cultural, and economic significance*

- *Creative, best friend says I am always seeing things differently and in multiple ways than others, I like to see things and get the full picture, leave no stone unturned, and get excited about any kind of new project*

267

Ancillary Skills

- *Public Speaking, am always comfortable speaking with others and can talk on a stage, in front of friends, or even enemies with ease and respect, can make up what I'm going to say on the fly or enjoy writing things down ahead of time*

- *Crafting, building things, am always working on a new project, focus on wood and metal mediums*

- *Technology, brother says I am pretty constantly looking into new tech devices and plans for where technology is leading the future, keep myself up to date on newest inventions and products and theories yet to be realized*

Primary Selling Point possibilities...

- *Teaching, creating videos, books, blogs, etc about current vents or history?*

- *Talking, podcasts, interviews, public voice?*

- *Creating, using crafts, selling on platforms, could somehow incorporate current events?...*

Once you have your profile of qualities, it will be time to move onto step number two, which is researching your different options for personal branding.

- Research different types of personal brands and decide on one for yourself.

As we have mentioned before in this book, there are different levels and types of personal branding, and each is ideal for a particular set of goals you would like to achieve. The most simple and common form of personal branding is inter-personal branding, wherein you curate a persona and social accounts for the people in your personal life, such as friends and family. While this initial thought may same deceptive or sociopathic, it really is just a slightly more concentrated effort to do what we have all been taught to do since day one of our existence here on Earth. We do not say certain things to others because of how it may make us look, we do not flaunt or open up about our flaws until we get to know others well. Essentially, inter-personal branding is just taking our natural tendencies one step further and giving our social lives more attention. This could involve fine-tuning and polishing your social media accounts to have a cohesive theme and professional aesthetic. You could quite easily tailor your personal style to be a bit more cohesive if it isn't already. You would most likely decide to be slightly more reserved than perhaps you used to be or others you know currently are, choosing to only present the best of your positive traits when initially meeting or talking with other people. After reading what inter-personal branding looks like, you may have just now realized you have been doing this all along, as have many people you know and love. It is such a common practice some people may even be totally oblivious to its existence. The practice of inter-personal branding will, however, be essential when moving on to more intense styles of personal branding in 2019.

The next level of personal branding is professional personal branding. Essentially, this type of branding is for when a person wishes to simply take their professional skill set and self-package it with their professional skills in order to appeal more desirable to potential or current employers. When creating this type of personal brand, one would simply add more profession-related content to their already curated personal social media accounts, such as posting articles related to work subject matter and posting pictures of themselves in more professional settings, giving their audience the impression that they are passionate about and dedicated to their work. A person seeking to cultivate their professional personal branding would also seek to highlight their personal attributes well, the same way they would have at level one. Some even decide to take it a step further and seek out opportunities to publish information or create content related to their field, so that when interviewing with or submitting resumes to potential employers, they can provide them with links to their various contributions and appear more educated and relevant in the area of work. Most using professional personal branding would also decide to create profiles for professional networking sites, such as LinkedIn. This type of branding is ideal for any working professional today, as it will absolutely help anyone to achieve greater employability and pay rates. As we discussed earlier in the book when addressing why personal branding is so important, we were reminded that *anyone* can match your qualifications, experience, and skillset. People you are competing with for a job may even have similar personal attributes. What will set you apart from the completion, however, is which of you puts forth more effort in presenting your career and self as the best possible option for the task at hand. While you already know and understand how important personal branding is in 2019, many people are still unaware of how personal branding techniques will help them flourish, so the odds are very much in your favor that you could perhaps be one of the only candidates in any job you apply for that is actively curating themselves and their careers for professional advancement.

The highest level of personal branding is, well, just called personal branding. It is what most people think of when they think about what personal branding is, as the lower two levels are essentially only partially utilizing personal branding techniques. Personal branding in its fullest form is when you package your personality, face, name, aesthetic, social accounts, and skill set to market to the broader public eye. This type of personal branding requires the most effort and work, but can also quite often reap the most reward. Many people who set out to turn their lives in recognized brands find some degree of recognition in the public eye and success either online or in other media outlets. Those who chose this type of personal branding often have to create content that is very innovative, creative, and entertaining as the markets for things such as books, movies, YouTube videos, and social media content are currently overflowing with new creators every day. The purpose of personal branding is to set yourself apart from these other creators and be able to cultivate a following that will supply enough revenue to live off of, and once you begin to experience some successes will hopefully be enough to fund the launching of new streams of revenue and ventures. If you are having difficulty picturing examples of personal branding based careers, there are plenty of notable examples all around you. We have already mentioned Martha Stewart and her ability to go from cook to billionaire. Kim Kardashian simply used her aesthetic, name, and personality to create a brand so popular she has now delved into makeup, fashions, and modeling. Even many notable

YouTube creators such as Shane Dawson, Jeffree Starr, and Simply Nailogical have become household names from creating online videos and have begun their own product lines in their respective areas of clothing and makeup.

Now that you have an understanding of the three different levels of personal branding, you need to examine your current lifestyle and what you want your future to look like. While a lot of people may say that full-on personal branding is clearly the best option for your life, only you will have to live with the decision you make the subsequent outcomes. Take the time to sit down and examine your familial and social obligations. Do you have a spouse and children that will need your financial and time-related support? Do you have an active and rich social life that really only working a normal 9-5 job will help you to maintain? Where do you want to be 5 years from now? How about 10 years from now? At the end of the day, only one of these options will best suit the life you want to live and the needs of those involved in your life. During this time you will also to have to be realistic about what you can and cannot achieve. Through personal branding, anyone can become more noteworthy and achieve much greater success than they would have before. Many, many skills and attributes are translatable into creation mediums, even if you may initially not believe them to be applicable to the fullest level of personal branding. However, you also have to take into consideration the market saturation of whatever it is you are wanting to market your personal brand is. It will be more difficult to become a YouTube beauty guru in 2019 than it was even five years ago. You have to be able to recognize your strengths and come up with creative ways you can utilize them to fulfill the level of branding that you desire. Personal branding is not a guarantee of success, but rather a tool you use that is guaranteed to *help* you succeed if you put in the time and work.

- Set goals.

When delving into a new personal branding venture, no matter what level you aspire to

276

compete, you need to set goals for yourself so that you can feel a sense of accomplishment to keep you motivated, stay focused on the task at hand, and be able to track your ongoing progress. Setting goals will help you stay focused. This is because you will have a set list, right in front of your very eyes, that will remind you of all of the things you have yet to overcome but will also help those things seem less daunting. I mean, if they can fit on a piece of paper or board, they can't be that scary, can they? They also help you to feel a sense of accomplishment because you are able to cross things off as you go and be reassured that you have not wasted your time or talent. This is also how you are going to be able to gauge your ongoing progress and be able to prove to yourself and to others that your hard work was worth it. Setting goals will also help you to gauge what is and is not realistic in your journey and will help you to more clearly see the outcome of all of your hard work. Goals can either be big or small, so long as they are specific, timed, and realistically achievable with the time and resources allotted to

277

them. Setting goals will be like having your own personal checklist of the major hurdles you are going to overcome, and it can be very helpful to understand everything that it left for you to accomplish, as well as serve as a pleasant reminder of all of the things you've already accomplished.

Setting goals is not making a checklist for your life plan. Rather, it is the checklist you make so that you can *create* a life plan. It helps you to keep a 'big-picture' perspective, even when things seem most difficult. Every person's goals will be different but goals, in general, tend to land in one of the different categories. Personal goals are goals that you set to accomplish within your personal life, such as how you interact with family or setting a number of new friends to make. When it comes to personal branding goals, people can set their eyes on many accomplishments depending on what level of branding you are going for. If you want to make a professional brand, you could set a goal that you will create 3 new blog posts or articles in the next month relating to your field. If you are seeking a full-forced personal brand, you could set period goals for reaching numbers of followers to your social accounts or views to your videos or publishers to send your book. In order to get a good sense of what setting goals really looks like, let us take a look at our example profile from earlier.

Name: John Smith, age 30

Personality Traits

- *Funny, mom said I am always making her laugh with jokes. A coworker said that I crack him up at our lunch break. A sense of humor is sarcastic, observational. Tend to poke fun at others without hurting feelings or going too far. Spouse says I make the most jokes about myself when in private.*

- *Informed, always researching current events and both sides of political arguments, can repeat that information back to others and am passionate about doing so, can process information and incorporate historical, cultural, and economic significance*

- *Creative, best friend says I am always seeing things differently and in multiple ways than others, I like to see things and get the full picture, leave no stone unturned, and get excited about any kind of new project*

Ancillary Skills

- *Public Speaking, am always comfortable speaking with others and can talk on a stage, in front of friends, or even enemies with ease and respect, can make up what I'm going to say on the fly or enjoy writing things down ahead of time*

- *Crafting, building things, am always working on a new project, focus on wood and metal mediums*

- *Technology, brother says I am pretty constantly looking into new tech devices and plans for where technology is leading the future, keep myself up to date on newest inventions and products and theories yet to be realized*

Primary Selling Point possibilities...

- *Teaching, creating videos, books, blogs, etc... about current events or history?*

- *Talking, podcasts, interviews, public voice?*

- *Creating, using crafts, selling on platforms, could somehow incorporate current events?*

Type of personal branding creating*: full-level. Want to create a YouTube channel where I make artwork based off of current events and topics affecting our society, maybe some historical pieces as well. Will also use social media and website to market and sell my artwork.*

As you can see here, John has decided to seek a full-level personal brand due to his qualifications. He had a knowledge and skill set that he could use to create content online and artwork in real life that very few people had seen before. He does have a spouse who is able to support them financially while he establishes his presence and works on his videos. He does not have experience making or editing content but is confident he could learn due to his love for tech. He is beginning to think about where this career could take him and is starting to set goals. He understands that further on in the process of creating his personal brand these goals may fluctuate or change, but he feels he needs a clearer picture and timeline of what exactly he is going to be working towards.

Goals in the next month...

- *Make Twitter, Instagram, Facebook, and YouTube accounts geared towards my artwork and current events*

- *Decide on a physical look for myself and brand*

- *Set up a website to begin selling my pieces of work*

- *Install video software and learn how to create intriguing videos*

- *Publish adds across social sites to attract followers*

- *Publish my first video*

- *Start a hashtag for my work #johntheartistspeaks, #johnsmiththinks, etc...*

Goals in the next six months...

- *Continue making a new video and piece of work every week*

- *Reach out to other YouTube creators who focus on political issues, current events, history and introduce them to my work and see about a collaboration*

- *Reach out to podcasts that focus on artists and or news and see about a collaboration*

- *Reach out to other social media influencers to see if they would be interested in collaborations or following my work*

- *Publish adds across social sites to get more followers*

- *Set up a blog and or website that takes an in-depth look at the issue or historical piece I am focusing on each week*

- *Submit my portfolio of work to be nominated for awards that I could qualify for and notify media reporting outlets of my work and nominations*

Goals in the next year...

- *Reach out to publishers, submitting pictures of my work and see about publishing a book of photos from my work and behind the scenes*

- *Try and book an appearance or interview on television or online media*

- *Get involved in activism and find a cause to create a series of work based on*

- *Reach out to companies that make tools and products I use for sponsorship for my videos and perhaps a marketing deal for their products*

- *Have my Facebook followers, YouTube subscribers, twitter followers, and Instagram followers all exceed 100,000*

- *Create merchandise featuring pictures of his artwork and quotes*

As you can see, while all of the details of his plan are not firmly cemented, he now has a clear picture of where he wants his career to take him. You too can create a clear vision for yourself and your personal brand by creating a list of goals similar to the one John made, only catered to your specific wants and needs. Do not be afraid to change this list as certain possibilities become better opportunities and other opportunities fade off or become irrelevant. If you still need guidance as to what you realistically can and cannot achieve, try researching examples of people whom you admire. Then go on to take a very in-depth look at their career and how they were able to get to the place you want to be. What resources did they have that you do? Which resources did they have that you could get? What was it that attracted people to them in the first place? What was different about what they were doing that landed them in the place they are in right now?

- Identify your audience.

We will be discussing how to define your audience more in-depth at a later point in the book, however, it is the next step you will need to do when starting your own personal brand. If you are seeking to create and inter-personal brand, then your audience would be friends and family. If you wish to cultivate a professional-brand then your audience is potential employers or current employers in your field. When seeking to create a new and full personal brand for yourself, then defining your audience becomes a bit more complex. You have to conduct some market research and find out what people, living in what areas, and from which age group and economic statues your content and brand would most appeal to. These categories could range anywhere from teenage girls on the west coast to middle-aged housewives in New England. While there is no formula for personal taste, demographic and market research data exists for a reason; so that people who want to market what they are selling to others can use their limited resources more efficiently. When running an ad on Facebook, for example, you do not want to pay money so that it is sent to people who would have no interest in what you are doing.

Let us again look at our example of John Smith. He is currently working on setting up a personal brand focused on combining art, news, history, and content creation to bring things to the attention of the public and sell his real-life work. His videos are styled with drama and dark color schemes, only allowing light to illuminate his works and the hands that create it. Over a lapsed period of time you begin to see the world he creates take shape, and listen to poetic and sadly sweet music. He includes links in his descriptions so that you can earn more about his work or the event he brings to life. While many people are bound to find this interesting, market research suggests that his target audience is not, in fact, teenage girls or teenagers in general. His work is also less likely to be sold or watched in places such as the South East as many of the events he chooses might be perceived as pro-liberal or anti-conservative. Elderly folk is also less likely to enjoy what he is doing as it is an abstract interpretation and less popular than the art and content they are used to. Research also suggests that people over the age of 65 are less likely to have accounts or be as active with their accounts anyway. So when he goes to publish ads or market his work, he chooses to select men and women from age 20-50, living in the Pacific Northwest, Southwest, and New England regions. He also uses keywords to refine their interests such as art, news, current events, politics, and crafts. This ensures that his advertisements go to people who will actually be likely to watch his content and buy his products when they see his ad.

Market research and knowing his audience will also help John to not change what he does in order to cater to people outside of his target demographic. Just as we discussed earlier, Martha Stewart does not use canned cranberry sauce because she knows her audience would rather make it from scratch because yes, they have the time and the money. If people want quick and affordable recipes they can make they can watch Sara's Weeknight Meals. Defining your audience helps you to remain focused and better target those who will contribute to your profits.

- Find your team.

No one can create a personal brand alone. You will need a team of people to help support you and guide you through this process. Those who help you emotionally could include anyone from friends or family. These people could even help you gain resources and can invest financially or with their time in helping you to launch your brand. You will need people to be there for you when the trials come and you feel like giving up. Let the people closest to you know how important it is to you that you make it in this career field and that your brand succeeds. If they are truly there for you unconditionally they should be your cheerleader no matter what. Those who could be your support system on a purely professional level would include people such as coworkers, colleagues, and mentors. We will discuss the importance of mentors later on in the book, but for now, you should understand that mentors are essentially people who have been where you are and can help you to navigate the things they had to learn for themselves or from their mentors. Coworkers and colleagues will help you by being a listening ear that will understand what you are going through, and you will each have something you can offer each other. This could be solid advice, new tricks or techniques they just discovered, or even collaborations for videos or projects. Your team will the rock on which you build and support your house, and you'll need them to be there for you, even if at times you just simply need to know that someone *is* there for you.

- Identify and gather your resources.

Resources are essentially anything that you can use to further your brand and accomplish your goals. The common school of thought is that there are three types of resources; time, talent, and treasure. Your time is any tie that you and your team members invest in building your personal brand. In order to evaluate what kind of time investment you can make, you must look at your current lifestyle and the availability of your team members. If you work a 9-5 job and do not intend on giving it up when launching your personal brand, you have to understand that you will have to invest more talent and treasure into your venture to make up for that deficit. In regard to talent, you have already taken stock of this resource before beginning this process. Factor it into your profile as a reminder of what you have going for you.

Finally, when you evaluate your treasure, this can

include money as well as material possessions. Things such as the technology you've already invested in, the software you have purchased, your new wardrobe, they all contribute to the amount of treasure you have to contribute to your personal brand. Investing your material wealth, however, involves a greater risk than your time or talent, as if you fail in your new branding efforts because you did not put in the work, you can still walk away with your talent and while your time is gone, you are given new time every day. Your wealth is the only investment you cannot recover, so you must be sure to take the time to examine what wealth you are willing to sacrifice to things such as video investments, product lines, or advertisements. To get a better picture, let us take a look at what John found when taking stock of his personal investments.

Time...

- *Left my day job,*

- *Family obligations and household duties take up several hours a day*

- *Overall, have about 12 hours a day to contribute*

- *My spouse is willing to help me set up accounts, check their progress, and even contact collaboration partners for me*

- *Colleagues have offered to help me spread the word about my channels and work*

Talent...

- *Skilled craftsman*

- *Creative*

- *Thoughtful*

- *Enjoy teaching others about the world and politics*

Treasure...

- *My spouse is able to pay the monthly expenses for several months until I start seeing revenue*

- *I already own a cell phone and have purchased another. My laptop is now equipped to edit videos, and I have purchased studio lighting, voice recording equipment*

- *Have affordable art supplies and a supplier to get more when needed*

- *Have a new wardrobe that appears artsy but serious*

- *Have a nest egg to invest in ads and opportunities*

You may look at John's list of resources and realize you can't quite match all of his blessings. However every person has been given some things that they could invest into a personal branding effort, and you just have to examine where your resources are and gather them together to truly ensure that your personal brand is going to be an available option for you at the moment. There is no shame in acknowledging that you may have to put your goals off for a period of time while you save money and other treasures to invest in your personal brand, or perhaps you may have to wait until you reach a point in your life that you can invest more time and energy into your reaching your goals. So long as you understand that personal branding is your best option for your future, the techniques will still be waiting here for you to implement further down the road. It is worthy to note, however, that the market for your particular persona and talent may not still be vacant in the future, as if there is a gap in the market, there is always someone eager to fill it. Remember this and try to do your best to accomplish your goals sooner rather than later.

- Make a schedule.

Yes, your parents and teachers were right all

throughout grade school; you need to budget your time! Your time is clearly a valuable resource, and unlike when we were younger, our time as adults is much more limited. We have houses to clean, kids to feed and drive pretty much everywhere, spouses to woo and jobs to go to. Your time will almost always slip away from you unless you make a concentrated effort to plan your days and nights ahead of time, and, this is the most important part, STICK TO YOUR SCHEDULE. You have wasted even more of your time if you have made a schedule and not stuck to it. At this point, you have hopefully had an honest review of your lifestyle and what type of personal branding you can realistically achieve in accordance with your other priorities, and also have some idea of the amount of time you can invest in your endeavors. This is the perfect time to buy a planner with sets spaces for days, weeks, and months so that you can take just 30 minutes at the beginning of each week to help you better budget your time. Sit next to your family calendar and fill in all of those plans and obligations first, followed by social calls and house maintenance. You may not enjoy this next part, but at this point, you may have to consider cutting certain things if you are unable to find sufficient amounts of time to build your personal brand. See which friend you could push until the weekend or the date night you could reschedule. Every life needs balance, and those closest to you will understand that you are trying to build a better life for yourself and the ones you love.

- Begin pouring your foundation.

At this point, you have identified what you have to offer the world. You know which type of personal branding you want to pursue and have set goals for your new career that is just brimming with possibilities. You have identified your target audience and have the best team possible on your side. You have a gathering of resources to use as needed, and a schedule to help you stay on track. It is finally time to begin the tangible work of creating your personal brand. This means finally changing your social media accounts (more information on that found in chapters 7-11), dressing in your new wardrobe, and creating content for your audience. This could mean making videos, posting pictures, or simply making informed articles and blog posts. You can also revamp your resume to include your new ventures and go out of your way to find new opportunities to invest your time into and places to market your personal brand. Whether it be a craft, trade skill, or simply persona that you are packaging along with your name and personality, it is time for the world to get to experience everything that you have to offer. Keep this step by step guide as a reference so that you can continue to come back to it as needed.

Chapter Five: The Importance of Being Yourself

The basis and foundation of your entire personal brand is *you*. People expect you to be unique but also to be relatable. This is why it's so important that you not only be yourself but be the *best* version of yourself that you can be. When marketing and self-packaging your own unique style, consumers, employers, and people in your personal life alike are able to tell when the behavior that you give them is genuine or fake. One of the most important qualities human beings can have and one of the best qualities that people tend to look for is honesty and realness. People will not buy what you were selling if they don't believe it is real and comes from a genuine place inside yourself. Over the course of history, many misguided entrepreneurs have believed that lying or deception are good ways to sell products. While unfortunately sometimes these people do see success, this kind of mindset is detrimental to the idea of personal branding. This is because unlike products, your personal brand cannot simply be redesigned or repackaged and resold by a different company. Your personal brand is you, your name and your face, all of which are vitally important to your overall personal brand and cannot be changed.

One thing the average person absolutely loves to hear is it the celebrity, icon, or professional that they see on TV, print media, or on social media is really just the same in real life as they are in the media that they present to others. One of the most disheartening things people can find out is that their hero, or that a personal brand that they love to follow, is truly unlike what they are presenting to the world. This kind of revelation can even be fatal to a personal brand, especially if most of your personal brand is not based on a talent or skill but rather the attributes and personality that you present to others. As we discussed earlier, Martha Stewart was able to become the largely successful mogul that she is today because of her overall unique style and pleasant presentation. On that same note, she became irreplaceable in her field and thus had a stronger personal brand that could survive the hurdles that all people who market themselves as brands may eventually face.

This is another reason why it is so important to be not only yourself but *uniquely* yourself. While we were all raised to believe that we were each a unique little snowflake, in the adult world it may be a lot harder than we realized to differentiate ourselves from others. When building a personal brand, it is essential that you identify what separates you from the rest of the crowd especially if you are pursuing a career in media content creation or are one of many people with your particular set of skills and talent. This is why the top entrepreneurs who have successfully marketed personal brands recommend that before starting your personal brand, you take the time to sit down and evaluate your own special personality traits and those things about yourself that attract others to you. This can be done in a variety of ways but many believe the best way to do this is 2 take just a few hours and have an honest conversation with yourself about your life thus far. Take this time to try and identify patterns that you've seen all the way from early childhood until now. Are you someone who frequently goes out of your way to help others? Do you often serve as a listening and caring ear to others? Are you able to converse with other people in a comfortable and energetic manner? Or maybe are you able to debate others and get your information across with conviction and passion? What words best describe you? Are you smart, funny, kind, or caring? Are you dedicated to your job or are you highly passionate about a certain field or area? These are all things that you can use to market your personality and or skill in the best way possible.

After you've been able to identify several key positive traits that you believe other people would like to see from you that you already possess, it is a very good idea to now approach those who know you best in your life and get their opinions. Ask them what three words would best describe you, and if those words do not match up with your own list or your own idea of what you believe your personal brand should reflect then perhaps ask them what you could be doing better to achieve different results. Ask other people, such as friends, family, co-workers or other people you socialize with regularly what kind of behavior patterns they see from you. Do they see that you're always taking a moment to help out your friends even when it means less time to do things for yourself? Or maybe do they see that you tend to be quick to anger and have a bit of a short temper that you could improve upon before trying to Market yourself as a whole?

Ultimately, when you were creating and building a personal brand, your ultimate goal is to sell that brand to others. These quote on quote 'others' would include people just like your friends just like your family just like your co-workers and just like the other people you socialize with. So no matter how close they are to the situation or how much you believe you need to take their opinion with a grain of salt, you have to come to accept and even celebrate the fact that their opinions will very much help you along this journey. When building a personal brand or even maintaining one, there is a definite propensity by many people to try and take on qualities that aren't true of themselves. Let us say for example that one quality you really admire but don't really have yourself is a selfless spirit It's not that you're selfish per say, it's just that you don't tend to find it easy to always be considering the opinions of others before you consider the opinions or needs of yourself. While trying to be a decent human being, in general, is always a good thing, trying to build your entire brand around the idea that you are selfless is just a recipe for disaster. It may be a quality that you want and that someday you may have, however, if you do not possess that quality a great deal right now, then it would be false to try and market your brand and your persona as having that quality. We all have areas in which we thrive in areas in which we can just survive. There is no shame in admitting that you have shortcomings and rather than focusing on your shortcomings, you should take the time to focus on your positive qualities and what makes you great. Once you've identified these areas, then your focus should be on amplifying those behaviors.

Being honest also entails ensuring that the skills, experience, and ideas you claim to possess are in fact true. We have all been guilty of padding or embellishing the truth now and again. Regardless of the moral implications of doing this, the professional repercussions will be severe. When you are under scorn or judgment from a potential employer or the public eye, things done in the dark will always come to light. People will find out that you only spent 1 year at La Cordon Blue instead of 2. Someone will know that the work order you got wasn't really from a top-paying client, but rather from your parent's friends. If you are willing to stand in your truth and market yourself as you are, then people will be willing to accept that you are not perfect. If your positive qualities are good enough and the content you create entertaining enough, often people do not even care about your experience or income or status in your field. Just take a moment to remember all of the people who simply got their start in careers on social media. They did not attend Harvard business school and yet they may now be more successful than someone who did. Even Instagram accounts for dogs get more followers than accountants, because I mean, of course, why wouldn't they? Take some comfort in knowing that even if you fail at starting a personal brand due to some unforeseen factor, you have a second chance so long as you have a corgi. Be honest about yourself and who you are, and there will still be an audience that wants to buy what you are selling.

Chapter Six: Defining Your Audience

As we discussed earlier, defining your audience is essential to creating your own personal brand. It is the process of examining your body of work and what you have to offer, followed by an intense dive into market research and what it tells you about how well or poorly you and your content will sell among different demographics. Defining your audience also entails conducting your own personal research as well as introducing common sense into the equation. You do not have to pay a market research analyst money to figure out that your fashion blog geared towards LGBTQIA youth is not going to circulate well in the over 65 communities of Boca Raton, Florida. While every person is an individual and it can seem cold or even heartless and sociopathic to boil people down to demographics and age ranges and taste, but at the end of the day it is not going to be worth your limited time and resources to market to an entire community for the sake of reaching your snowflake consumer.

Defining your audience is also essential because as you may already know, once you have a defined your group of interest and best possible marketing opportunities, you can now begin to target that audience with your branding. This can mean running ads in media that you know members of your key demographic are likely to tune in to, as well as deciding to research the ways in which you can better serve the people who will hopefully become your financial supporters. Let us say, for example, that you are targeting men and women in their 30's and 40's who are interested in cooking. You create a cooking channel on YouTube and write a weekly blog about all things happening in the kitchen. Since you know who will be most likely to tune into your channel, read your blogs, and follow you on social media, you should consider what kinds of things people in this age range and demographic enjoy most. Your recipes are made from simple ingredients and sometimes premade things, so you know that your target audience is most likely people who work and do not have a great deal of time or money to spend on every meal, but still want to make them taste good and be nutritious. You could write several posts periodically about the importance of balancing time with quality preparation in the kitchen. You could make sure to use less professional techniques and make your videos easy to follow and recreate at home. You could partner with brands that are available in the lesser-expensive grocery stores when sponsoring products or having videos paid for.

Ultimately, defining your audience will help you to conduct a better, more targeted effort in your personal brand, and it simply involves identifying your audience, then getting to know them and the things that they value, then implementing that into your branding technique. You can even cater to your audience without compromising yourself in professional branding. Yes, it is somewhat more difficult to know what a potential employer wants as they do not publish market research reports on such things, but you can deduce what type of things they are looking for simply by getting to know more about the company. Read their website and memorize their company values. If you have the time, prior to an interview or submitting a resume, include some of those keywords into your social media posts. See what kinds of coworkers they have hired. Are there any common traits you see? Get to know what your potential employer wants to see and hear from an ideal candidate, and do your best to implement that into your own brand and delivery. Defining your audience is simply identifying who is most likely to buy what you are branding, and then giving them what they would like most. Learn to empathize with your audience and make them feel comfortable when taking in everything you have to offer.

Chapter Seven: Personal Branding with Facebook

Personal branding on Facebook is key, no matter what your ultimate goals for personal branding are. In order to build your brand on Facebook, you will have to first create a personal account. If you already have one, then you can simply revamp it under the following guidelines.

- Make your profile picture clean and professional- NO SELFIES OR MIRROR SHOTS. It is a good idea to invest in some professional pictures in multiple outfits from a real photographer and have them sent to your computer.

- Choose a color scheme, as well as a background or 'banner' photo that perfectly encapsulates the 'feeling of you'. Example: if your brand is focused on clean living and exercise, choose a stock photo of exercise equipment, a counter full of fruits and vegetables, etc...Make it relevant, clean, and not too specific

- Begin posting pictures and messages daily, if not multiple times a day. Clear pout any personal photos you already have on your account, no matter how personal. You want your page to appear professional and curated, not as if you are just another random person. Post clean, interesting photos of yourself and, if relevant, your loved ones. Refrain from personal messages to friends or family on your page- only things relating to your brand should go on your homepage

- Create interesting content by posting inspirational memes, links to articles related to your brand, make videos and do live streams

- Connect with others related to your field, join groups to get yourself known

- Pictures of yourself can be dramatic, sexy (within reason), artsy, relevant, advertisements, pics of you smiling, laughing, or faux candid pictures.

- Pictures of yourself cannot be: selfies, blurry, with poor lighting, in street clothes, with un-styled hair or makeup, controversial, political or religious (unless your brand is involved with politics or religion), advertised without saying they are advertisements

If this is your first time making a Facebook page, then you need to recruit friends, and fast. Search for anyone you know and begin reaching out to them on Facebook and hope that they friend you back. You could even get out old yearbooks and go name by name. You will not be using this account for personal reasons so security is not an issue. The more friends you have the more popular you seem, so get your friend count higher quickly.

If you have a business component to your brand, such as our example John who was selling his artwork, you also need to create a business Facebook page. Curate it in a similar way to your personal account, only with more pictures of your work or product. From here, you can create ads and 'boost posts' to targeted demographics and audiences and have them run for specific days to attract more buyers and generate more word of mouth for your brand. Be sure to include a picture of yourself in your post! This may be the first time people see your brand, so use interesting, clear and crisp photos.

Chapter Eight: Personal Branding on Instagram

Personal branding on Instagram is very similar to branding on Facebook. You will need to follow all of the previous guidelines for how to create an account or clear out your current account. If Instagram is your main vessel for storing pictures, consider creating a new account and changing the name on your current account to a nickname or something else people would recognize you by so your full name can be used for your personal brand. You could even consider coming up with a cool and relevant nickname for your brand if you desire.

With Instagram, however, you will be in search of followers, and unlike like Facebook, Instagram does not have a friend request option. Followers are only brought to you if THEY want to follow you, regardless of whether or not you follow them. So try reaching out to friends and family in real life and asking them to follow you. Then the people who follow them will see your profile in their recommendations. You could also create an ad for your account on Instagram. However, it must be a business page and you must also have a Facebook business page to do so. Once you do, however, you will have five different options for creating and running an ad, including photos, videos, conversions, and outreach. Each ad is tailored to a demographic and unlike Facebook, you cannot ignore Instagram ads, as you have to scroll past them in order to see more photos on your page. Instagram stars garner big followings by creating very interesting content such as videos in under 60 seconds, and their followers share their videos across other platforms. Encourage those you know and your followers to share your content so that you can reach more people, and remember the picture guidelines from chapter seven!

Chapter Nine: Personal Branding on YouTube

YouTube is a video publishing platform that, while many of us have accounts on, not many of us publish videos there. Even if you do not want a career based on YouTube, you can still use it to your advantage for advancing your personal brand. When creating videos, make sure they are well lit, have clear sound, and edited well. Search for video editing software that will fit your budget and computer operating system requirements. Make a unique and styled channel page with color schemes, fonts, and relevant pictures. Create a short video introducing your channel and telling people about the video you'll be posting to it and why. From then on, publish videos at least once every week, preferably on the same day and time, if not more often. While the specifics of videos you make will vary depending on your personal brand, you can always be sure that your content does not include swear words, sexual content, or immoral actions or you could face demonetization, wherein you will not make money off of your videos. Anyone with a YouTube account and the funds can create ads to get your video more views, which do not count until the viewer has watched for at 30 seconds. Try connecting with other YouTube stars as they are a close-knit community and often collaborate together and support each other.

Chapter Ten: Personal Branding with Twitter

Twitter is the least customizable yet somehow most personal of all social media platforms. You can create an account using your nicest profile picture and can choose a background image for your page. However and pictures you post will only be listed as a hyperlink in your text body, and can be viewed only as part of an album featured on your page. Twitter is best used, then, for sending out thoughts, messages, and links to other relevant materials or content. Twitter is fast and simple to use, although it is still recommended you clear out all of your old tweets so your new or revamped account is seemingly professional. Try and share only positive thoughts and comments, or things only relevant to your brand. People's biggest source of unease and bitterness in 2019 is reading hurtful or negative things online, so refrain from posting such things on your accounts. Send out tweets regularly with reminders of upcoming events or projects, and you can even 'live-tweet' events and inform followers of how things are going. Try to use professional but familiar language, and start off by again recruiting the people you know to follow you. Try following random strangers and see if they will follow you back. You can create ads on Twitter to boost the audience of who sees your post, but it will be pinned as 'promoted' when people see it so they will know it was paid for. Avoid getting into rants, fights, or long-standing feuds with people to avoid looking divisive, and be sure to follow the picture and video guidelines set forth in previous chapters.

Chapter Eleven: Having Mentorships

A mentor is an essential part of the personal branding process. A mentor is someone who will help to guide you through the highs and lows of the personal branding journey, giving you key pieces of advice and resources. At this point you may be asking yourself 'Ok, but how on Earth do I find one?". Basically, a mentor is an experienced professional in your field who has built their own successful personal brand or has been the working force behind the personal brand of someone else. While anyone with a successful personal branding career will be a great resource of help and guidance for you, typically you should begin the search for a mentor by looking at people with careers and results similar to what you want to achieve. For example, if you wanted to create a food based YouTube channel, you could reach out to the creator of the popular channel Binging With Babish. Not only does he has millions of followers, but he has also created a unique and easy to follow set up and is one of the few YouTube stars who is consistent with video delivery dates. Many personal brands have professional business emails attached to them, either featured on their website, in video descriptions, or on social media biographies. It is a good idea to contact a wide range of possible mentors, as chances are that anyone with a successful full-force personal brand is going to be busy and unable to respond to you. Try contacting at least 50 people, and although you may want to have a Martha Stewart level career, do not waste your time reaching out to any celebrities. Contact lesser-known authors, video creators, etc...as they will be more likely to help you. A great portion of finding a mentor is trying to connect to people's heartstrings and hope that they will see your talent and value your vision enough to take the time to help you.

Having a mentor is also quite possible, and perhaps even easier to find, when you are seeking to build yourself a personal brand solely in the realm of a professional career. You can take the time to research other working professionals who perhaps have the job that you are hoping to get, or perhaps have an even higher or more coveted position. These professionals could be found online by searching through company directories on websites or even looking through profiles on LinkedIn. Again, you will want to reach out to multiple people as some may not respond to you, however, the chances are much more likely that they will, even if it is just to thank you for your time and tell you they are unavailable. If you do receive multiple offers to guide you, however, take hold of every opportunity. Chances are that most mentors will not be staying in your life for a long period of time, so be willing to stretch yourself thin for a short period of time in order to absorb the most knowledge and wisdom from those who have made it to where you want to be. Once you have one, or even several, experienced people willing to give you their time and attention, it may feel overwhelming or confusing as to what to ask them. So start out by creating an interview style list of questions, wherein you ask anyone who is willing to help you the same set of rudimentary questions, such as "How did you accomplish this?", "What technology do you use?", or "How long did this take?". You may find different answers than you expected, and it will begin to give you a more accurate gauge of what you can expect going into the process of building a personal brand or yourself. Ultimately, your mentor will someone you can keep in your life to ask all of the questions you may find you need to be answered along the way, and with any luck, they will admire your tenacity and courage and will do their best to help you succeed.

Chapter Twelve: How to Monitor Your Personal Brand

You have now created multiple social media accounts, set realistic goals, and have started to market yourself and what you have to offer the world. You have contacted valuable people and gathered the resources you will need to succeed. You have begun creating content and have found a receptive audience for what you are doing. Your main focus now is to achieve the goals that you have set in a timely manner and to start bringing in revenue through one of the multiple streams, such as creating personal merchandise, sponsoring products, getting ad sponsorships, or receiving views and likes on monetized videos. Now that the wheel of your personal branding journey have started turning and you have found your foundation to be solid, you may be asking yourself where exactly do I go from here? Am I going to be successful or unsuccessful because I do or don't achieve some of my goals? Exactly how do I measure and gauge my success so I can determine whether or not this has all been worth it?

Well, the first step in monitoring the progress of your personal brand is to start by examining the solid numbers you can find across your platforms. On your social media accounts, keep track of the number of followers you have as well as likes and comments. In theory, this number should be growing over the course of your career, seeing higher boosts after things such as collaborations or interviews. Next, you can view the number of views on videos and blog posts, as well as see if people are reading or purchasing other content you have created, such as magazines, books, or online letters. The tangible numbers and how much revenue you are taking in will be the best ways to easily gauge your progress as time goes on. However, there are others ways than numbers to measure your successes. For example, you can factor into the worth of your brand how it makes you feel to be working in the field. Is it much more difficult and stressful than you thought, or do you enjoy your work on a daily basis? You can also consider how many resources you have put into your efforts and how many resources you are receiving in return. Are you at a substantial loss, are you making a profit, or are you breaking even? Just as with any business, you need to know the answer to this question at any given time and need to make changes if the results are not what you would like for them to be.

You can also monitor the success of your personal brand by assessing how many new opportunities you are able to get over the course of your career. Are you being approached to sell or endorse products, or are you being asked to do collaborations? Have you gotten the attention of publishers or other influential people in your field of work or in the media? If the answer is no, perhaps you can begin rethinking your strategy and start working to actively garner more opportunities for publicity and revenue. If you were only personal branding for the sake of bettering your job opportunities or promotions, then your progress can be monitored by simply whether or not you got those new opportunities. It is very important that, regardless of what level of branding you are pursuing, that you actively ensure you are maintaining your social accounts and other outlets as those who post infrequently lose followers and therefore lose opportunities. Ultimately, monitoring your brand is simply asking yourself the questions of where you think you ought to be by now, and then actually reviewing where you are and gauging how well the two line up. If they do not, you now know you need to change your methodology and approach. If they do, you know that you need to continue doing what works and work towards creating an even better career. A good idea is to have these 'check-ins' periodically, and how often they occur is really up to you, though anything more than once a month is unnecessary. Monitoring your brand is essentially checking in with your career so that you can tailor the results of your work to fit the needs of your life.

Conclusion

Thank for making it through to the end of *Personal Branding in 2019,* and let's hope it was informative and able to provide you with all of the tools you need to achieve your goals whatever it is that they may be. Just because you've finished this book doesn't mean there is nothing left to learn on the topic, and expanding your horizons is the only way to find the mastery you seek.

The next step is to begin researching other successful personal brands and why they interest you. Take the time to get an understanding of why they are successful. Then go on to complete the personal branding foundation checklist, realizing what you have to offer the world and how you can utilize what makes you unique and valuable to begin a long and fulfilling career.

Continue to research possible mentors and idols, as well as new or innovative techniques and brands that you could admire and incorporate into your own efforts. Remember to take an honest and accurate gauge of the resources that are available to you, and use them with care and responsibility. When beginning to build your personal brand, remember to always be yourself and make an active and purposeful effort to curate a unique, styled, and marketable brand and image that will sell your persona and skills. No one else can be Martha Stewart, and no one else can be YOU.

Finally, if you found this book useful in any way, a review on Amazon is always appreciated!

Made in the USA
Lexington, KY
21 May 2019